THE BEST OF
Andrew Murray

120 Daily Devotions

TO NURTURE YOUR SPIRIT AND
REFRESH YOUR SOUL

Editor's note: The selections in this book have been "gently modernized" for today's reader. Words, phrases, and sentence structure have been updated for readability and clarity; new chapter headings and Scripture verses have been combined with excerpts from Andrew Murray's text. Every effort has been made to preserve the integrity and intent of Murray's original writings. Reflection questions at the end of each reading have been included to aid in personal exploration and group discussion.

The Best of Andrew Murray
ISBN: 979-8-88898-146-7 - *Paperback*
ISBN: 979-8-88898-147-4 - *Hardcover*
ISBN: 979-8-88898-148-1 - *Ebook*

Copyright © 2024 by Honor Books
Racine, WI

Edited and complied by Stephen W. Sorenson.
Cover design by Faille Schmitz.

ABOUT ANDREW MURRAY

Calling Believers to a Deep, Intimate, Christian Life

One of the most revered ministers and writers of his day, Andrew Murray (1828-1917) spent his life calling believers to uncompromising holiness, reliance on the Holy Spirit, and an ever-deepening relationship with the heavenly Father.

The second of four children horn to Andrew Sr. and Maria Murray, Andrew Murray was raised in what was considered then the most remote corner of the world—Graaff-Reinet, South Africa. At the age of ten, he was sent to Scotland for formal education, followed by three years of theological study in Holland. Murray returned to South Africa to minister in revival meetings, social and educational mission work, and devotional writing.

Murray's first pastorate was in Bloemfontein, a sparse and isolated territory of nearly 50,000 square miles and 12,000 people beyond the Orange River. His gifts were soon recognized and appreciated, and in the years ahead he went on to become a leader in the Dutch Reformed Church, shepherding several large and influential churches. As a preacher, he consistently drew huge crowds and led many to Christ. Later, he was used by God to lead a revival that swept through South Africa.

But Murray's life was not without hardship. He endured adversity and affliction, which refined his faith and gave him deeper insight into God's nature. As a young man, a prolonged illness left him frail and exhausted. Later, in the prime of his ministry, severe sickness forced him to leave the pulpit for two years.

God used these difficulties to further mold Murray's attitude and heart. As his daughter recalled, "It was after the 'time of silence' [sickness] when God came so near to father and he saw more clearly the meaning of a life full of surrender and simple faith. He began to show in all relationships that constant tenderness and unruffled loving-kindness and unselfish thought for others which characterized his life from that point. At the same time, he lost nothing of his strength and determination."

The father of nine children, Murray, along with his wife, Emma, ministered to an endless stream of people who came and went through his household. In 1873, he helped to establish the Huguenot Seminary, a school that trained young women for educational work. He also served as the first president of the Young Men's Christian Association (YMCA).

Used powerfully during his lifetime to spur revival and movements of the Holy Spirit, Murray's legacy of faith continues today through his vast array of writings. Indeed, he is considered one of the most insightful, inspiring, and prolific Christian authors of the past few centuries. Among his numerous widely read books are *With Christ in the School of Prayer, Absolute Surrender, Abide in Christ, Waiting on God*, and *The True Vine.*

Throughout his life, Andrew Murray's prayer was, "May not a single moment of my life be spent outside the light, love, and joy of God's presence and not a moment without the entire surrender of myself as a vessel for Him to fill full of His Spirit and His love." Few would deny that his prayers were answered, as his total dedication and devotion to God remain an inspiration to Christians around the world.

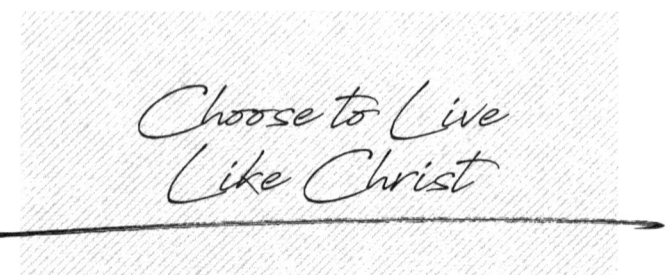

Choose to Live Like Christ

"He who says he abides in Him ought himself
also to walk just as He walked."

1 John 2:6

When Jesus redeemed us with His blood and presented us to the Father in His righteousness, He did not leave us in our old nature to serve God as best we could. No, in Him dwelled the eternal life, the divine life of heaven. Everyone who is in Him receives from Him that same eternal life in its holy heavenly power. So nothing can be more natural than the claim that the person who abides in Jesus, continually receiving life from Him, must also walk as He walked.

This mighty life of God does not work as a blind force, compelling us ignorantly or involuntarily to act like Christ. On the contrary, walking like Him must come as a result of a deliberate choice, sought in strong desire, accepted by a living will.

When He calls us to abide in Him that we may receive that life more abundantly. He points us to His life on earth and tells us that the new life has been bestowed so we will walk as He walked. We are to think, speak, and act as Jesus did. As He was, so we are to be.

Reflection

What specifically does it mean to "walk like Christ" in daily life?

How can you more closely follow His example this week?

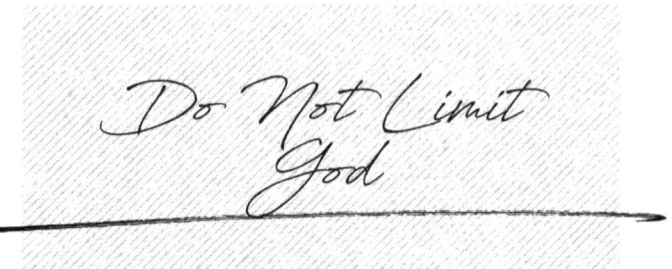

Do Not Limit God

"Now to Him who is able to do exceedingly abundantly above all that we ask or think, according to the power that works in us, to Him be glory."

Ephesians 3:20–21

God is able to do for us exceeding abundantly above what we ask or think—and yet we are in danger of limiting Him when we confine our desires and prayers to our own thoughts.

The Israelites show how people tend to place limitations on God's power. When Moses promised them meat in the wilderness, they doubted, saying, "Can God prepare a table in the wilderness? Behold, He struck the rock, so that the waters gushed out, and the streams overflowed. Can He give bread also? Can He provide meat for His people?" (Ps. 78:19-20). If they had been asked whether God could provide streams in the desert, they would have answered, "Yes!" God had done it; He could do it again. But when the thought came of God doing something new, they limited Him. Their expectation could not rise beyond their past experience or their thoughts of what was possible.

Likewise, we may be limiting God by our conceptions of what He has promised or is able to do. Let us beware of limiting the Holy One of Israel in our prayers. Let us believe that the very promises of God we plead have a divine meaning, infinitely beyond our thoughts of them. Let us believe that His fulfillment of them can be, in a power and an abundance of grace, beyond our largest grasp of thought

Reflection

In what ways do you limit God through your earthly perspective and thinking?

How can you "stretch" your thoughts to imagine what God can do?

God Looks at the Heart

"Let us draw near with a true heart."

Hebrews 10:22

In man's nature, the heart is the central power. As the heart is, so is the man. The desire and the choice, the love and the hatred of the heart prove what a man is already—and determine what lie wall become.

Just as we judge a man's physical character by his outward appearance, so the heart gives the real inward man his character. The hidden man of the heart is what God looks at.

True religion is a thing of the heart, an inward life. It is only as the desire of the heart is fixed on God, giving its love and finding its joy in God, that a man can draw near to God. The heart of man was expressly planned, created, and endowed with all its powers, that it might be capable of receiving and enjoying God and His love. A man can have no more of religion, holiness, love, salvation than lie has in his heart.

The true heart is nothing but true consecration, the spirit that longs to live wholly for God, that gladly gives up everything that it may live wholly for Him. Above all, the true heart yields itself up, as the key of the inner life, into His keeping and rule.

Reflection

Is your heart truly, fully yielded to God?

If not, what is keeping you from yielding it completely to Him?

God Has First Rights to Our Time

"What! Could you not watch with Me one hour?"

Matthew 26:40

How is it that some Christians say they cannot afford to spend a quarter hour or a half hour alone with God and His Word? We find time easily enough when we have to attend an important meeting or there is anything related to our advantage or pleasure.

Our great God, in His wondrous love, longs for us to spend time with Him so that He may communicate to us His power and grace. Even God's own servants, who might consider it their special privilege to spend much time with Him in prayer, are so occupied with their own work that they find little time for that which is all-important—waiting on God to receive power from on high.

Dear child of God, let us never say, "I have no time for God." Let the Holy Spirit teach us that the most important and the most profitable time of the whole day is the time we spend alone with God. Communion with God through His Word and prayer is as indispensable to us as the bread we eat and the air we breathe. Whatever else is left undone, God has the first and chief right to our time. Only then will our surrender to God's will be full and unreserved.

Reflection

How much time do you spend with God?

How might you arrange your schedule so you can spend more time waiting on Him and receive the blessings He wants to give you?

Live a Blessed Life of Love

> "Beloved, if God so loved us, we also ought
> to love one another."
>
> *1 John 4:11*

The same Spirit who said, "Consider Christ Jesus—take time, and give attention to know Him well," says to us, "Consider one another—take time, and give attention to know the needs of people around you." How many are there whose circumstances are unfavorable, whose knowledge is limited, whose entire lives are hopeless, that there is little prospect of their ever attaining a better life? For them, there is but one thing to be done: we who arc strong ought to bear the infirmities of the weak. Each one who begins to see the blessedness there is of a life fully surrendered to Christ should offer himself to Christ, to be made His messenger to the feeble and weary.

Love and good works are to be the aim of the church in the exercise of its fellowship. Every thing that can hinder love is to be sacrificed and set aside. Everything that can promote and persuade and provoke others to love is to be studied and performed. And along with love, good works, too.

The church has been redeemed by Christ, to prove to the world the power He has to cleanse from sin, to conquer evil, to restore to holiness and to goodness. Let us consider one another, in every possible way to promote love and good works.

Reflection

What can you do to promote love in the church?

How can you show love to someone who is facing great challenges?

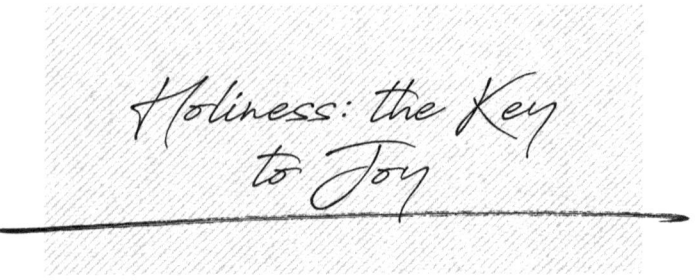

Holiness: the Key to Joy

"The disciples were filled with joy and with
the Holy Spirit."

Acts 13:52

If you would have joy—the full, abiding joy that
nothing can take away—strive to be holy as God
is holy. Holiness is blessedness. Nothing can
darken or interrupt our joy but sin. Whatever trial or
temptation we face, the joy of Jesus can more than compensate and outweigh. As Peter said, "Though now you
do not see Him, yet believing, you rejoice with joy inexpressible" (1 Peter 1:8).

Let us glory in Him who is our holiness, for in His
presence is fullness of joy. Study to understand the divine
value of joy. It is the evidence of your being in the Fathers
presence and dwelling in His love. It is the proof of
being consciously free from the law and the strain of the
spirit of bondage. It is the token of your freedom from
care and responsibility because you are rejoicing in Christ
Jesus as your sanctification and your strength. It is the
secret of spiritual health and vitality, filling all your
service with the happy, childlike assurance that the Father
asks nothing that He does not give strength for, and that
He accepts all that is done in this spirit.

There is nothing so attractive as joy. And what is the

secret of being joyful? It is the desire and the discipline to pursue holiness

Reflection

Why is joy so attractive?
Would people who know you well say that you are joyful?
If not, how might sin be affecting your joy?

Finding Perfect Rest

"Come to Me, all you who labor and are
heavy laden, and I will give you rest . . . For
My yoke is easy and My burden is light."

Matthew 11:28,30

The secret of perfect rest is entire surrender to Jesus. Giving up one's whole life to Him, submitting to Him and taught by Him, and abiding in Him—these are the conditions of discipleship without which there can be no thought of maintaining the rest that was bestow'ed when you first came to Christ. Rest is in Christ and not something He gives apart from Himself.

Because so main young believers fail to lay hold of this truth, rest speedily passes away. They did not know how, when Jesus said, "My yoke is easy," He spoke the truth. Just the yoke gives the rest, because the moment the soul yields itself to obey, the Lord gives the strength and joy to do it. They did not notice how, when He said, "Learn from Me," He added, "I am gentle and lowly in heart." They did not know that when He said, "Abide in Me," He only asked for the surrender to Himself.

These two, surrender and faith, are the essential elements of the Christian life—giving up all to Jesus and receiving all from Him.

Reflection

How do you obtain perfect rest in Christ?

What steps might you take to draw closer to Him?

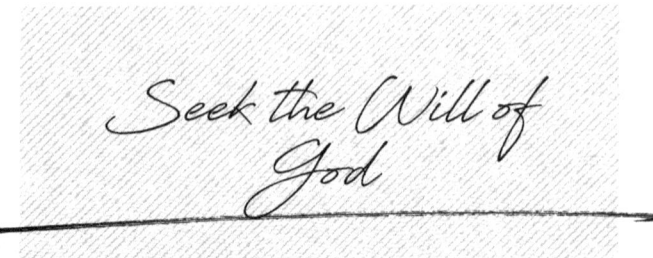

Seek the Will of God

"Yet indeed I also count all things loss . . .
that I may know Him and the power of His
resurrection, and the fellowship of His
sufferings, being conformed to His death."

Philippians 3:8, 10

The way of death is the way of life. The only way to be set free from our fallen nature, with the curse and power of sin resting on it, is to die to it. Jesus denied Himself and would do nothing to please the nature He had taken on, sinless though it was in Him. He denied it; He died to it.

Jesus gave up His own will to seek nothing but the will of God. That was to Him the path of life. And this is to us the living way. Accept God's will in every situation. Obey Gods will in every command of nature as His word. Seek God's perfect will in every leading of His Spirit. Say, "I have come to do your will, O God." Let God's wall be the one aim of your life. It will be to us as it was to Him, though it leads through death—the path to God and to life.

As we know Christ in the power of His resurrection, He leads us into conformity to His death. He does it in the power of the Holy Spirit. His death and His life work in us, and we are borne along on the wall of God to where He is.

Reflection

What does "conformity to His death" mean?

How deeply do you desire God's will rather than your own?

When Your Joy in Christ Wanes

"Abide in Me."

John 15:4

To you who have heard and paid attention to the call, "Come to Me," this new invitation comes from the same loving Savior: "Abide in Me." You doubtless have never regretted coming when He called. You experienced His Word as the truth. All His promises He fulfilled. He made you partakers of the blessing and joy of His love. Was not His welcome most hearty, His pardon full and free, His love most sweet and precious?

Yet you have had to complain of disappointment; as time went on, your expectations were not realized. The blessings you once enjoyed were lost. The love and joy of your first meeting with your Savior, instead of deepening, have become faint and feeble. Often you have wondered why your experience of salvation should not have been fuller.

The answer is simple: You wandered from Him. The blessings He bestows are all connected with His "Come to Me" and are only to be enjoyed in close fellowship with Him. You did not fully understand, or did not rightly remember, that the call meant, "Come to Me and stay with Me." Yet this was indeed His object and purpose when He first called you to Himself. It was not to refresh you for a few short hours after your conversion with the joy of His love and deliverance, and then to send you forth to wander in sadness and sin.

No, indeed. He had prepared for you an abiding dwelling with Himself, where your whole life and every moment of it might be spent, the work of your daily life might be done, and all the while you might be enjoying unbroken communion with Him.

Who would, after seeking the King's palace, be content to stand in the doorway when he is invited to dwell in the King's presence and share with Him in all the glory of His royal life? Oh, let us enter in and abide, and enjoy to the fullest all the rich supply His wondrous love has prepared for us!

Reflection

What does it mean to "abide" in Christ?

Think about your relationship with Him and how satisfied you are in that relationship. What has disappointed you in your spiritual walk?

What hope does God offer you?

Imitating Christ in Suffering

"For this is commendable, if because of
conscience toward God one endures grief,
suffering wrongfully. For what credit is it if,
when you are beaten for your faults, you take it
patiently? But when you do good and suffer, if you
take it patiently, this is commendable before God."

1 Peter 2:19–20

I n our sinful nature, there is more faith in might and right than in the heavenly power of love. But the person who would be like Christ must follow Him in this also: He seeks to conquer evil with good. The more another does him wrong, the more he feels called to love him. Even if it be necessary for the public welfare that justice should punish the offender, he takes care that there is no motive of personal vengeance. As far as he is concerned, he forgives and loves.

Ah, what a difference it would make in our churches and our testimony to the world if Christ's example were followed, if each one who was reviled "did not revile in return," if each one who suffered "did not threaten, but committed Himself to Him who judges righteously" (1 Peter 2:23). Fellow Christians, this is literally what the Father would have us do.

In ordinary Christian life, where we mostly seek to fulfill our calling as redeemed ones in our own strength, conformity to the Lord's image is impossible. But in a life of full surrender, where we have given all into His hands, the glorious expectation is awakened that the imitation of Christ in this area is indeed within our reach.

Reflection

What changes would occur in our churches if each Christian, when treated poorly, responded in a patient and forgiving way through the power of God?

In what ways have you acted vindictively toward someone who first hurt you?

How would God have wanted you to respond toward that person?

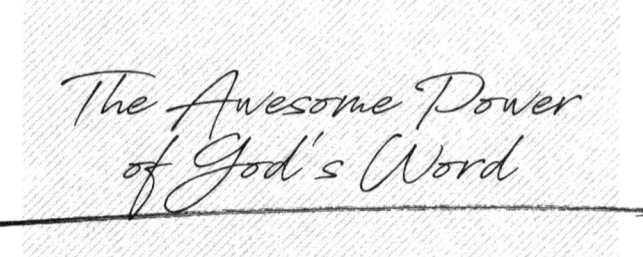

The Awesome Power of God's Word

By His Word, God "calls those things which do not exist as though they did" (Rom. 4:17). As true as this is of all Gods mighty deeds (rom creation to the resurrection of the dead, it is also true of every word spoken to us in His holy hook.

The Word is the power of God for salvation; it supplies everything we need. All the treasures and blessings of God's grace are within our reach. The Word has power to enlighten our darkness. Into our hearts it will bring the light of God and knowledge of His will. The Word can fill us with courage to conquer every enemy and strength to accomplish whatever God asks us to do. The Word would cleanse, sanctify, and become in us the seed of every trait in the likeness of our Lord. Through the Word, the Spirit leads us into all truth—that is, it makes all that is in the Word true in us and so prepares our heart to be the dwelling place of the Father and the Son.

Let us begin our training for that ministry of the Word by proving its power in our own experience. Let us begin to seek this, quietly committing ourselves to learn the great faith lesson—the mighty power of God's Word.

Reflection

In what ways have you seen the power of Gods Word come alive in your life?

What will you do this week to discover more of God's Word and its life-changing blessings?

What a Difference God's Love Can Make

"And now abide faith, hope, love, these three;
but the greatest of these is love."

1 Corinthians 13:13

O Christian, study what love is. Study it in the Word, in Christ, in God. See Him as an ever-flowing fountain of all goodness, who has His very being and glory in this—that He lives in all that exists and communicates to all people His own blessedness and perfection. As you understand that God is the source of love, you will recognize that anyone who doesn't love has not known God. And you will learn, too, to admit that no effort of your will can bring forth love. It must be given to you from above.

God has the power to instill His love in our hearts by the Holy Spirit given to us. He has promised to give Christ dwelling in our hearts by faith so that we will be rooted and grounded in love, and know and have in us something of a love that passes knowledge.

What a difference it would make in the world if every believer were to give himself with his whole heart to live for his fellow men! What a difference it would make to his own life, as he yields himself to God's saving love in its striving for souls! What a difference it would make to all the Christian ministries that suffer for want of devoted, wholehearted helpers! What a difference it would make to our churches, as they grew to know what they have been gathered for! What a difference it would make to thousands of spiritually lost people, who would wonder at the love that is in God's children—what power and blessing there is in that love

Reflection

What difference would it make if you made it your priority to be a student of God's love?

Where does genuine love come from, and how can you learn more about it?

The Heart of Biblical Meditation

"I will meditate on Your precepts, And
contemplate Your ways."

Psalm 119:15

I n meditation, the heart holds and appropriates
the Word of God. Just as in reflection the1 understanding grasps all the meaning and bearings
of a truth, so in meditation the heart assimilates it and
makes it a part of its own life. The meditation of the
heart implies desire, acceptance, surrender, and love. Out
of the heart spring the issues of life—what the heart
truly believes, what it receives with love and joy, what it
allows to master and rule the life. The intellect gathers
and prepares the food we are to eat. In meditation, the
heart takes it in and absorbs it.

Another element of true meditation is quiet restful-
ness. In our study of Scripture, our intellect often needs
to put forth its utmost efforts. The habit of soul required
in meditation is different. Here we turn with some truth
we have found or some mystery in which we are waiting
for the Holy Spirit to reveal its meaning and power in
our inner life.

In meditation, personal application takes a prominent
place. This is all too seldom the case with our intellectual
study of the Bible. Its object is to know and understand.

In meditation, the chief object is to ingest and experience. A readiness to believe even promise implicitly, to obey every command unhesitatingly, to "stand perfect and complete in all the will of God," is the only true spirit of Bible study. It is in quiet meditation that this faith is exercised. Through meditation, the full surrender to all God's will is made, and the assurance of grace is received to perform our vows.

Reflection

Are you satisfied with the amount of time you meditate on God's Word and His ways?

If not, how can you devote more time and energy to this discipline?

Why is biblical meditation so important—and yet so often overlooked?

Meditation and Prayer: A Vital Connection

"How sweet are Your words to my taste,
Sweeter than honey to my mouth!"

Psalm 119:103

Meditation must lead to prayer. It provides matter for prayer. It must lead on to prayer, to ask for and receive definitely what it has seen in the Word or accepted in the Word. Its value is that it is the preparation for prayer, deliberate and whole-hearted supplication for what the heart has felt the Word has revealed as needful or possible.

The reward of resting for a time from intellectual effort, and cultivating the habit of holy meditation, will be that during the course of time the two will be brought into harmony, and all our study will be animated by the spirit of a quiet waiting on God and a yielding up of the heart and life to the Word.

Our fellowship with God is meant for all the day. The blessing of securing a habit of true meditation during the morning devotions will be that we will be brought nearer the blessedness of the man mentioned in the first psalm: "Blessed is the man [whose] delight is in the law of the Lord, and in His law he meditates day and night" (Ps. 1:2).

Let nothing less be your prayer and expectation, that your meditation may be true worship, the living surrender of the heart to God's Word in His presence. Make the words of the psalmist your highest aim and sincerest prayer: "Let the words of my mouth and the meditation of my heart be acceptable in Your sight, O Lord, my strength and my Redeemer" (Ps. 19:14).

Reflection

What is the connection between prayer and meditation?

How do the two disciplines complement each other?

Ask God to help you nurture the habit of praying as you meditate on His Word.

Let God Work in You

"He who has begun a good work in you will
complete it until the day of Jesus Christ."

Philippians 1:6

Every believer is in Christ, but not every one abides in Him—in the consciously joyful and trustful surrender of the whole being to His influence. Abiding in Him is to consent with our whole soul to His being our life, to reckon upon Him to inspire us in all that goes to make up life, and then to give up everything most absolutely for Him to reign in us. It is the rest of the full assurance that He does, each moment, work in us what we are to be. He enables us to maintain that perfect surrender in which He is free to do all His wall.

Let all who indeed long to walk like Christ take courage at the thought of who He is and who He wall prove Himself to be if they trust Him. He is the True Vine; no vane ever did so fully for its branches what He will do for us. We have only to consent to be branches. Honor Him by a joyful trust that He is, beyond all conception, the True Vine, holding you by His almighty strength, supplying you from His infinite fullness.

Reflection

To what extent do you really trust Christ?

What kinds of things, including feelings, can cause us to doubt that He really will meet our needs?

How can we stay focused on who Christ is and His promises to us?

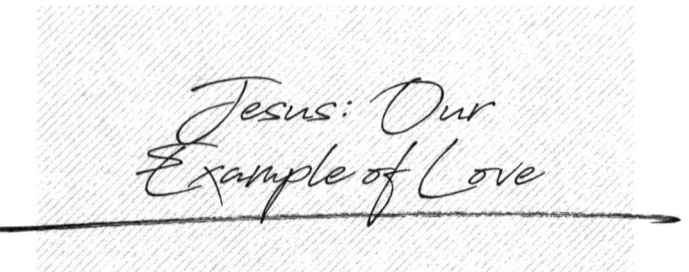

Jesus: Our Example of Love

"I have given you an example, that you
should do as I have done to you."

John 13:15

Jesus Christ does indeed ask every one of us always to act just as we have seen Him act. What He has done for us, and still does each day, we are to do over again to others. He is our example; each of us is to be the copy and image of the Master.

When we look on Jesus—His obedience to the will of the Father, His love as manifested in the sacrifice of Himself—we see the most wondrous and glorious thing heaven has to show. In heaven itself, we will see nothing greater or brighter. Surely such an example given by God on purpose to make the imitation attractive and possible ought to win us. Is that not enough to stir all that is within us with a holy jealousy and with joy unimaginable?

It is not the remembrance of what Jesus has once done for me, but the living experience of what He is doing now for me, that will give me the power to act like Him. His love must be a present reality, the inflowing of a life and a power in which I can love like Him. It is only by the Holy Spirit I realize what Jesus is doing for me, and how He does it. Only by the Spirit's power is it possible to do to others what He is doing for me.

Reflection

Pray that the love
and power of Jesus
will fill you and
enable you to love
others the way He
loves you.

The Life–Changing Power of Servanthood

"For even the Son of Man did not come to be
served, but to serve, and to give His life a
ransom for many."

Mark 10:45

I n taking the form of a servant, Jesus established
the law of rank in the church of Christ. The
higher one wishes to stand in grace, the more it
must be his joy to be a servant of all. If I seek to bless
others, it must be in the humble, loving readiness with
which I serve them, not caring for my own honor or
interest.

The reason why we so often do not bless others is
that we wish to address them as their superiors in grace
or gifts—or at least their equals. If we first learned from
our Lord to associate with others in a spirit of servant-
hood, what a blessing we would become to the world!
When this attitude and practice become customary within
the church of Christ, the power of His presence will
soon make itself felt.

The follower of Jesus makes the salvation of the soul
the first object in his ministry of love—at the same time
seeking to reach others by the ready service of love in
the little and common things of daily life. It is not by
reproof and censure that he shows he is a servant. Believers become living witnesses of God's love through

the friendliness and kindness with which they carry out daily interactions. From such a person, a word of testimony comes with power and persuasion.

Reflection

When is it most difficult for you to be a servant to others?

Ask God to help you understand what it means to be a living witness for Him.

Then think about three practical and natural ways in which you can serve people you know who aren't yet Christians.

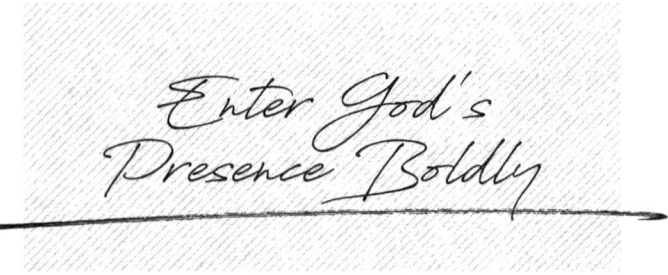

Enter God's Presence Boldly

"Now in Christ Jesus you who once were far off have been brought near by the blood of Christ."

Ephesians 2:13

T he blood of Jesus was poured out in a death that perfectly fulfilled God's will and was a mighty victory over all the temptations of sin and self.

Beloved Christian, think what the blood of Jesus, the blood of the Lamb, means! God gave it for your redemption. God accepted it when His son entered heaven and presented it on your behalf. God has it forever in His sight as the fruit, the infinitely well-pleasing proof, of His Son's obedience unto death. God points you to it and asks you to believe in the divine satisfaction it gives Him, in its omnipotent energy, in its everlasting sufficiency.

Will you not this day believe that Jesus' blood gives you liberty, confidence, and boldness to enter into the very presence of the everlasting God? Go this very moment with the utmost confidence and take your place in the most intimate fellowship with God. And if your heart condemns you, or coldness or unbelief appear to make a real entrance impossible, don't rest until you believe and fully prove the power of the blood in every deed to bring you near.

Reflection

What has the power
of Jesus' blood
accomplished in
you?

How will you
respond to the
fellowship God
offers you?

Knowing Your Mission

"We are ambassadors for Christ."

2 Corinthians 5:20

It is a great help if an ambassador knows clearly what his mission is, that he has nothing to do but accomplish it, and that he has given himself undividedly to do this one thing. For the Christian, it is no less important that he should know that he has a mission, what its nature is, and how he is to accomplish it.

Every Christian must be the image of Jesus—must demonstrate the same love to sinners and desire for their salvation that animated Christ—that the world may know what Christ is like. Whoever you are and wherever you live, the Lord has chosen you to be His representative in the circle in which you move. He has fixed His heart on you and saved you, in order that you will exhibit to those around you the very image of His unseen glory.

Every believer may depend on it, that as the Father gave His Holy Spirit to the Son to fulfill His mission, so Jesus will give His people all the power and wisdom they need. The grace to show forth Christ always, to exhibit the lovely light of His example and likeness, is given to everyone who only heartily and resolutely takes up his heavenly calling.

Reflection

What is your mission as God's representative?

If you are not perfectly clear about the Lord's purpose for your life, how might you become more certain about it?

Power of the Resurrected Christ

"I have been crucified with Christ; it is no
longer I who live, but Christ lives in me; and
the life which I now live in the flesh I live by
faith in the Son of God, who loved me and
gave Himself for me."

Galatians 2:20

Through faith in Christ, we become partakers of His life. That life has passed through death on the cross, and the power of that death and resurrection is always working.

I have been crucified with Christ; I have crucified the flesh. I thus learn how perfectly I share in the finished work of Christ. If I am crucified and dead with Him, I am a partner in His life and victory. I learn to understand the position I must take to allow the power of that cross and that death to manifest itself in overcoming sin (see Romans 6:6).

There is still a great work for me to do. But that work is not to crucify myself. Scripture says I have been crucified; the "old man" was crucified. But I have always to regard and treat my old nature as crucified and not allow it to come down from the cross. I must maintain my crucified position.

Through my crucified Savior, I was freed from the life of the flesh. I received new life. Christ lives in me. The flesh, though condemned to die, is not yet dead. Now it is my calling, in the strength of the Lord, to see that the old nature is kept nailed to the cross.

Reflection

What is involved in keeping the old, sinful nature "nailed to the cross"?

Why is that so important?

When People Treat You Unjustly

"In this you greatly rejoice, though now for a
little while, if need be, you have been grieved
by various trials, that the genuineness of
your faith . . . may be found to praise, honor,
and glory at the revelation of Jesus Christ."

1 Peter 1:6–7

hrist believed that suffering was in the will of
God. He had found it in Scripture that the
servant of God should suffer, lie had made
Himself familiar with this thought, so that when suffering
came it did not take Him by surprise. He expected it. He
knew that through suffering He needed to be perfected.
So His first thought was not how to be delivered from
it, but how to glorify God in it. This enabled Ilim to hear
the greatest injustice quietly, for He saw God's hand in
it.

Christian, would you have the strength to endure
injustice and mistreatment in the spirit as Christ did?
Train yourself to recognize the hand of God in everything
that happens to you. This lesson is of more consequence
than you think. Whether it be some great wrong that is
done to you or some little offense that you meet in daily
life, before you fix your thoughts on the person who did
it, first be still and remind yourself, "God allows me to
come into this trouble to see if I will glorify Him in it.
This trial, be it the greatest or least, is allowed by God
and is His will concerning me." Seek to submit to God's

will in it. Then receive the wisdom to know how to behave during it.

With your eye turned from man to God, suffering wrong is not as hard as it seems. Meet every offense that man commits against you with the firm trust that God will watch over and care for you. Commit it to Him, who judges righteously.

Reflection

What injustice in your life, or the life of someone you love, do you need to submit to God's will?

How might the certainty that God is watching over you influence how you respond to the person committing the injustice?

Beware of Double-Mindedness

"Set your mind on things above, not on
things on the earth."

Colossians 3:2

God cannot at times hear the prayer of your lips because the worldly desires of your heart cry out to Him much more strongly and loudly. The life exercises a mighty influence over prayer. A self-seeking life makes prayer powerless and an answer impossible.

For many Christians, there is a conflict between the life and prayer, and life holds the upper hand. But prayer can also exercise a mighty influence over the life. If I give myself entirely to God in prayer, prayer can conquer the life of the flesh and sin. The entire life may be brought under the control of prayer. Prayer can change and renew the whole life because prayer calls in and receives the Holy Spirit to purify and sanctify.

Many think that they must, with their defective spiritual life, work themselves up to pray more. They do not understand that only in proportion as the spiritual life is strengthened can the prayer life increase. Prayer and life are inseparably linked.

Learn this great lesson: My prayer must rule my

whole life. What I request from God in prayer is not decided in five or ten minutes. I must learn to say, "I have prayed with my whole heart." What I desire from God must really fill my heart the whole day, then the way is open for a certain answer.

Reflection

How does a focus on worldly desires affect our prayers?

How do our prayers affect our worldly desires?

What do you think is meant by the phrase: "My prayer must rule my whole life"?

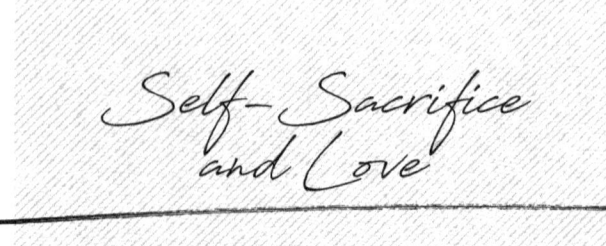

Self-Sacrifice and Love

"Be imitators of God as dear children. And walk in love, as Christ also has loved us and given Himself for us, an offering and a sacrifice to God for a sweet-smelling aroma."

Ephesians 5:1-2

The highest glory of God's love was manifested in the self-sacrifice of Christ. It is the highest glory of the Christian to be like his Lord in this same way. Without complete self-sacrifice, the new command—the command of love—cannot be fulfilled.

Let all your actions and conversation be, according to Christs example, saturated with love. This love made His sacrifice acceptable in God's sight, a sweet-smelling aroma. As His love exhibited itself in self-sacrifice, let your love prove itself to be like His in daily self-sacrifice for the welfare of others, so it will also be acceptable in God's sight.

For every Christian who gives himself entirely to His service, God has the same honor as He had for His Son; He uses him as an instrument of blessing to others. Therefore, John says, "He who does not love his brother whom he has seen, how can he love God whom he has not seen?" (1 John 4:20). The self-sacrifice in which you have devoted yourself to God's service binds you also to serve your fellow men.

Reflection

Which area of your
life requires the
greatest self-
sacrifice?

Why is self-sacrifice
essential in loving
as Christ loved?

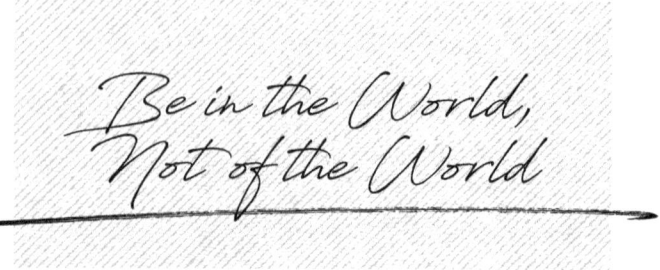

Be in the World, Not of the World

"I have given them Your word; and the world
has hated them because they are not of the
world, just as I am not of the world."

John 17:14

Some people have taken "not of the world" as their life motto. From the earliest ages, when people thought they had to escape to cloisters and deserts to serve God, to our own days when some seek to show their piety by harshly judging all that is in the world, there have been those who counted this the only true religion. There was separation from sin, but also no fellowship with sinners. The sinner could not feel that he was surrounded with the atmosphere of a tender heavenly love. It was a one-sided and therefore a defective religion.

Then there are those who, on the other side, embrace the words "in the world." They appeal to the words of the apostle, "Since then you would need to go out of the world" (1 Cor. 5:10). They think that by showing that religion does not make us unfriendly or unfit to enjoy all that there is to enjoy, they will induce the world to serve God. It has often happened that they have succeeded in making the world very religious, but at too high a price—religion became very worldly.

The true follower of Jesus must combine both. If he

does not clearly show that he is not of the world and prove the greater blessedness of a heavenly life, how will he convince the world that a better way exists? How will he prove that there is a higher life all can attain through Christ's love? Earnestness, holiness, and separation from the temptations of the world must be his aim. And yet he must live as one who is "in the world"—expressly placed here by God, among those who are of the world, to win their hearts, gain influence, and communicate to them the truths of Gods Word.

Reflection

How effective are you at balancing these perspectives? Where might you need to place more emphasis?

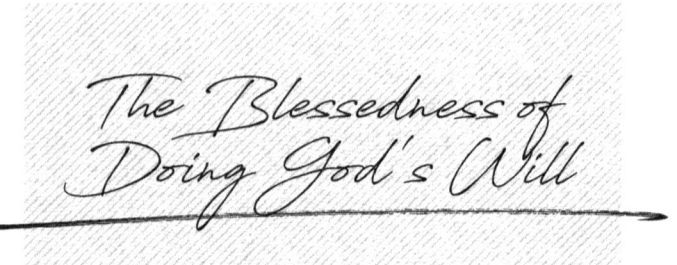

The Blessedness of Doing God's Will

> "For I have come down from heaven, not to
> do My own will, but the will of Him who
> sent Me."
>
> *John 6:38*

In all of nature, the will of God is done. In heaven, the angels find their highest blessedness in doing God's will. For this, man was created with a free will, in order that he might have the power to choose, and ol his own accord do God's will. Deceived by the devil, man committed the great sin of doing his own will rather than God's will. Yes, rather his own than God's will! In this is the root and wretchedness of sin.

Jesus Christ became man to bring us back to the blessedness of doing God's will. The great object of redemption was to make us and our will free from sin's power and to lead us again to live out the will of God. In His life on earth, Jesus showed us what it is to live only for the will of God. In His death and resurrection, He won for us the power to live and do God's will as He had done.

The believer who knows the power of Jesus' death and resurrection has the power to consecrate himself entirely to God's will. He knows that the call to follow' Christ means nothing less than to take and speak the words of the Master as his own solemn vow, "I seek not my own will, but the will of the Father."

To attain this, we must begin by taking the same stand that our Lord did. Take God's will as one great whole, as the only thing for which you live on earth. There is nothing that will bring us closer to God in union to Christ than loving, keeping, and doing the will of God.

Reflection

Why is it often difficult to live out the will of God in our lives? Ask God to show you what it means to live only to do His will rather than your own.

Cultivate Compassion

"But a certain Samaritan, as he journeyed, came where [the injured man] was. And when he saw him, he had compassion. So he went to him and bandaged his wounds, . . . set him on his own animal, brought him to an inn, and took care of him . . . Go and do likewise."

Luke 10:33–34, 37

Compassion is the spirit of love that is awakened by the sight of need or wretchedness. What abundant opportunities there are every day to practice this heavenly virtue, and what need there is for it in a world so full of misery and sin! Every Christian ought therefore by prayer and practice to cultivate a compassionate heart, as one of the most precious marks of likeness to the blessed Master.

Opportunities for showing compassion are all around us. There are the poor and sick, widows and orphans, distressed and despondent—people who need more than anything the refreshment a compassionate heart can bring. Pray earnestly for a compassionate heart, always ready to be an instrument of divine compassion. It was the compassionate sympathy of Jesus that attracted so many to Him on earth. That same compassionate tenderness wall still draw people to you and to your Lord.

Reflection

What inspires compassion in your heart?

In what ways can you demonstrate Christlike compassion to someone in your sphere of influence this week?

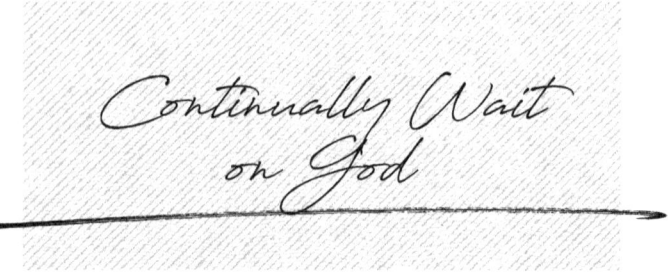

Continually Wait on God

"So you, by the help of your God, return;
observe mercy and justice, and wait on your
God continually."

Hosea 12:6

Continuity, unbroken and ceaseless, is essential to a healthy Christian life. Every moment, God wants me to be and waits to make me what He expects of me and what is well-pleasing in His sight. If waiting on God is the1 essence of true religion, maintaining the spirit of entire dependence must be continuous. The call to "wait on your God continually" must be accepted and obeyed.

In God's love, life, and work there can be no break, no interruption. Do not limit God in this by your thoughts of what may be expected. Fix your eyes on this one truth: In His very nature, God, as the only Giver of life, cannot do otherwise than work every moment in His child. Do not look only at the one side: "If I wait continually, God will work continually." No, look at the other side. Place God first and say, "God works continually; every moment I may wait on Him continually."

Reflection

What does it mean to "wait continually" on the Lord?

What steps can you take this week to spend more time with Him and participate in His continual work?

Reach Out in Love

"By this all will know that you are My
disciples, if you have love for one another."

John 13:35

J ust as Christ demonstrated God's love, believers are to demonstrate to the world Christ's love. They are to prove to men that Christ loses them and fills them with a love that is not of earth. They, by living and loving just as He did, are to be perpetual witnesses to the love that gave itself to die. Christ loved so that even the Jew s cried out, as at Bethany, "See how He loved him!" (John 11:36). Christians are to live so that people are compelled to say, "See how these Christians love one another."

Amidst all diversity ol character, creed, language, or station, Christians are to prove that love has made them members of one body. Love has taught them each to forget and sacrifice self for the sake of other people. Their life of love is the chief evidence of Christianity, the proof to the world that God sent Christ.

Let our life be one of self-sacrifice, always studying the welfare of others, finding our highest joy in blessing others. And let us, in studying the divine art of doing good, yield ourselves as obedient learners to the guidance of the Holy Spirit.

Reflection

Why will the love
of Christ stand out
in today's culture?

In what ways can
you demonstrate
this kind of love to
people around
you—in your
community, at work,
in your family?

Strength in Weakness

"My strength is made perfect in weakness."

2 Corinthians 12:9

T he Christian often tries to forget or deny his weakness. God wants us to remember it and feel it deeply. The Christian mourns over his weakness. Christ teaches His servant to say, "I take pleasure in infirmities; most gladly wall I glory in my infirmities." The Christian thinks his weakness is his greatest hindrance in the life and service of God. God tells us that it is the secret of strength and success.

Our whole life and calling as disciples find their origin and guarantee in these words: "All authority has been given to Me in heaven and on earth" (Matt. 28:18). What He does in and through us, He does with almighty power. What He claims or demands, He works Himself by that same power. All He gives, He gives with power. The weakest believer may be confident that in asking to be kept from sin and grow in holiness, he may count on his petitions being fulfilled with divine power.

The trusting believer lives a most joyous and blessed life, not because he has prevailed over weakness, but because, being utterly helpless, he knows the mighty Savior will work in him.

Reflection

How is Gods perspective on weakness different from ours?

Which weaknesses do you need to give to God so He can work mightily in and through you?

Hide Yourself in Christ

"Put off, concerning your former conduct, the
old man which grows corrupt according to
the deceitful lusts [and] put on the new man
which was created according to God, in true
righteousness and holiness."

Ephesians 4:22,24

U nless this life of self, with its willing and
working, is displaced by the life of Christ,
with His willing and working, to abide in
Him will be impossible. And then comes the solemn
question from Him who died on the cross: "Are you ready
to give up self to the death? You, the living person born
of God, are already dead to sin and alive to God. But are
you ready now, in the power of this death, to give up self
entirely to its death of the cross, to be kept there until
self is completely destroyed?"

Believer, if you would truly and fully abide in Christ,
prepare yourself to part forever from self and not allow
it, even for a single moment, to have anything to say in
your inner life. If you are willing to sacrifice self and
allow Jesus Christ to become your life within you, inspiring all your thinking, feeling, and acting, He is ready to
undertake the responsibility. In the fullest and widest
sense the word life can have, He wall be your life, extend-
ing His interest and influence to each of the thousand
things that make up your daily life.

Hide yourself in Christ. In Him alone is your safety.

He will teach you to be humble and watchful. He will teach you to be happy and contented. Trust Him to take the place that self once filled so easily and so naturally.

Reflection

Why must every Christian, in the power of the living Christ, win the battle over "the old man"—the sinful self?

Do you value Jesus Christ so highly that you will choose to allow Him to become the life within you?

If so, what steps will you take to do this?

Trust in God's Light

"The Lord make His face shine upon you, and
be gracious to you; the Lord lift up His
countenance upon you, and give you peace."

Numbers 6:25–26

E very morning, the sun rises and we walk in
its light and perform our daily duties with
gladness. Whether we think of it or not, the
sun's light shines on us all day. Every morning, the light
of God shines on His children. But in order to enjoy the
light of God's countenance, the soul must turn to God
and trust Him to let His light shine on it.

Begin each day with the words of the psalmist: "Lord,
lift up the light of Your countenance upon us . . . Make
Your face shine upon Your servant" (4:6; 31:16). Believe
that your Father ardently longs for you to dwell and
rejoice in His light all the day. Just as you need the light
of the sun each hour, so the heavenly light is indispensable.

Even when there are clouds, we still have the sun. In
the midst of difficulties, the light of God will rest on
you without ceasing. Make sure that the light of God
shines on you in the morning, and you can count on that
light being with you all the day.

Reflection

Start your day with prayer, inviting God to shine His light on you during all your day's activities.

And when difficulties arise, remember that God is still with you and rejoice in His blessings.

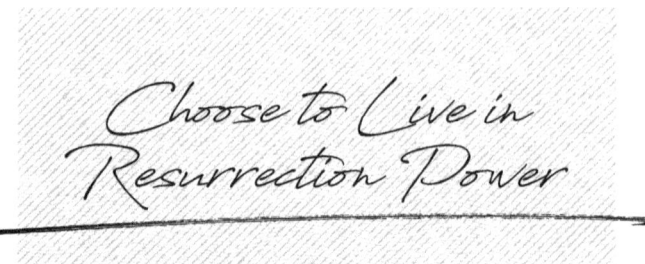

Choose to Live in Resurrection Power

"With great power the apostles gave witness
to the resurrection of the Lord Jesus."

Acts 4:33

Come, all you who are weary of a life unlike Jesus and long to walk always in His footsteps. In seeking your own will and glory instead of God's, you have seen how far you are from Jesus' obedience, humility, and love. And now the question is whether you are willing to say, "If Jesus will take possession of my life, I resign all right or wish ever to have or do my own will. I give my life with all I have and am entirely to Him, always to do what He through His Word and Spirit commands me."

The living Jesus, who is the resurrection, has shown His power over all our enemies. He, who so loves us, will work in us. He gives us the Holy Spirit as our power, and He will perform His work in us with divine faithfulness, if we will only trust Him.

Your calling is to live like Christ. To this end, you have already been made one with Him in the likeness of His resurrection. The only question is now whether you desire the fill experience of His resurrection life, whether you are willing to surrender your whole life so that He may manifest resurrection power in every part of it. I urge you not to draw back. Offer yourself unreservedly to Him, with all your weakness and unfaithfulness. Believe that He, the risen one, will still work in you exceedingly abundantly above all you could think or desire.

Reflection

Do you truly long to experience the resurrection life in Christ?

What prevents God from possessing your entire life?

How can you allow God to fully occupy the throne of your heart?

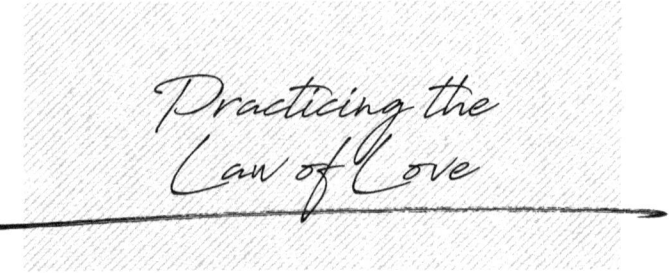

Practicing the Law of Love

"This is My commandment, that you love one another as I have loved you."

John 15:12

As I have loved you. This phrase gives us the measure of the love with which we must love each other. True love knows no measure; it gives itself entirely.

We who would be like Christ must unhesitatingly accept this as our rule of life. We know how difficult it often is to love people who are offensive or unpleasant. Therefore, before going to meet those who might test our ability to love, we must pray and seek to comprehend the love with which the Lord has loved us. We lay ourselves on the altar before the Lord, praying, "Even as You have loved me, so will I love other people."

Oh, that Christians would close their ears to all the reasonings of their own hearts and fix their eyes only on the law that He who loves them has declared by His own example. Then they would realize that there is nothing for them to do but to accept His commands and obey them. The love of Christ is no mere suggestion or sentiment; it is a law that can be fulfilled only through Gods power.

Reflection

Ponder God's deep love for you, which led Jesus to die on the cross for your sins.

Invite God to fill you with His powerful love and enable you to love other people— including those who are unpleasant and offensive—as He commands.

You Are God's Temple

"Do you not know that you are the temple of
God and that the Spirit of God dwells in
you? If anyone defiles the temple of God,
God will destroy him. For the temple of God
is holy, which temple you are."

1 Corinthians 3:16–17

From eternity, God desired to create man to be a dwelling in which to show forth His glory. Through man's sin, this plan seemingly failed. In His people Israel, God sought a means of carrying out His plan. He established a house in the midst of His people—first a tabernacle, then a temple—in which He could dwell. This was but a shadow and image of the true indwelling of God in redeemed mankind, who would be His temple to eternity. So we are "being built together for a dwelling place of God in the Spirit" (Eph. 2:22).

Meanwhile, since the Holy Spirit has been poured forth, God dwells in each heart that has been cleansed and renewed by the Spirit. The message comes to each believer: "Do you not know that you are the temple of God?" How little this truth is known or experienced, and yet how true it is.

Jesus once said, "If anyone loves Me, he will keep My word; and My Father will love him, and We will come to him and make Our home with him" (John 14:23). Through the Holy Spirit, you will be sanctified into a temple of God—your heart will be His home.

Reflection

What responsibilities are involved in being Gods holy temple, and why does God take these so seriously?

In what ways do these responsibilities conflict with the perspectives of our culture on personal freedom?

What role does obedience play in being God's temple?

Fellowship in the Spirit

"The communion of the Holy Spirit be with you all."

2 Corinthians 13:14

I t is the Holy Spirit through whom the Father and Son are one, and through whom they have fellowship with each other.

We communicate and commune with the Father and Son through the Spirit: "Our fellowship is with the Father and with His Son Jesus Christ" (1 John 1:3). As the Spirit enables us, we experience the fellowship of love in the life with the Father and Son.

Through the Spirit we, as God's children, have fellowship with one another. "There is one body and one Spirit" (Eph. 4:4). And through the Spirit, the unity of the body must be maintained.

One reason the Spirit does not work with greater power in the church is that the unity of the Spirit is too little sought after. In heaven, there is an eternal fellowship of love between the Father and Son through the Spirit. Let us offer ourselves to God, imploring Him to grant us the unity and the fellowship of the Spirit with all members of Christs Body.

Reflection

Why is unity among
the Body of Christ
essential?

What makes such
unity possible?

The Sign of True Discipleship

"Behold what manner of love the Father has
bestowed on us."

1 John 3:1

L ove is the explanation of the whole, awe-in-
spiring life of Christ and of the wonder of
His death. Divine love in God's children will
still work mighty wonders.

"See how He loved him!" (John 11:36). These words
are the superscription over the love of the Father and
the Son, and they must become key words in the life of
every Christian.

Beloved Christians, Christ Jesus longs to make you,
amidst those who surround you, a fountain of love. The
love of heaven would gladly take possession of you and
thus bless the world through you. Offer yourself unreservedly to its indwelling. Honor it by the confident
assurance that it can teach you to love as Jesus loved. As
conformity to Jesus must be the chief mark of your
Christian walk, so love must be the chief mark of that
conformity.

Don't be disheartened if you don't attain it at once.
Only keep firm hold of the command, "Love . . . as I have
loved you." It takes time to grow into it. Take time in

secret to gaze on that image of love. Take time in prayer and meditation to fan the desire for it into a burning flame.

Reflection

How committed are you to experiencing Jesus' love and sharing it with people around you?
Pray and meditate on love, and ask God to give you opportunities to share His love.

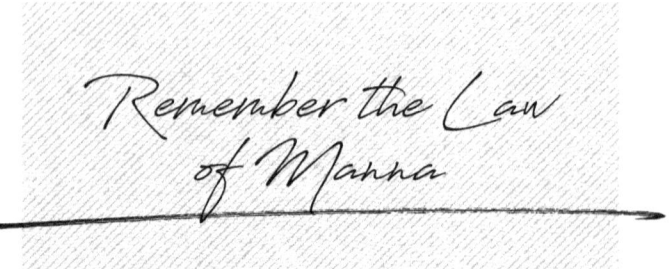

Remember the Law of Manna

"Now in the morning, having risen a long while before daylight, He went out and departed to a solitary place; and there He prayed."

Mark 1:35

Why did the Savior need hours of quiet, isolated prayer? Didn't He know the blessedness of silently lifting up His soul to God in the midst of the most pressing business? Didn't the Father dwell in Him? And didn't He in the depth of His heart enjoy unbroken communion with the Father?

Yes, He did indeed enjoy that rich, hidden life. But that life, being subject to the law of humanity, continually needed refreshing and renewing from the fountain. It was a life of dependence. Just because it was strong and true, it could not hear the loss of direct and constant communication with the Father.

What a lesson for every Christian! Nothing can atone for the loss of secret, intimate, and direct communication with God. It sustains and strengthens us. For even work in the service of God and of love is exhausting. We cannot bless others without power going out from us; this must be renewed from above.

Remember the law of manna: That which is heavenly

cannot remain good for long on earth but must day by day be renewed afresh from heaven. This still holds true today. Jesus Christ models it for us; every day, we need to have communion with our Father in secret. We are similar to Christ as He walked the earth—we need time day by day to be fed from heaven. It is from the Father alone that the power to lead a heavenly life on earth can come.

Reflection

What do you do to receive refreshment and renewal from God every day?

How is your life different when you aren't spiritually fed each day from heaven?

The More Abundant Life

"I have come that they may have life, and that
they may have it more abundantly."

John 10:10

All true Christians have received life from Christ. The majority of them, however, know nothing about the more abundant life that He is willing to bestow. Paul speaks constantly of this. He says about himself that the grace of God was "exceedingly abundant" (1 Tim. 1:14). He also says, "I can do all tilings through Christ who strengthens me" (Phil. 4:13). Paul echoes these themes over and over again.

We forget that the entire flesh, with all its affections, must be regarded as crucified and be handed over to death. We must not be satisfied with an ordinary life, but must seek an abundant life. We must surrender ourselves entirely, that the Spirit may take full possession of us, that there may come an entire transformation in our spiritual being.

What is it, then, that peculiarly constitutes this abundant life? The abundant life is nothing less than the full Jesus having the full mastery over our entire being, through the power of the Holy Spirit.

Reflection

Are you experiencing this abundant life?

If not, what is keeping you from seeking and experiencing it?

God Walks with Us

"God is our refuge and strength, a very present help in trouble. Therefore we will not fear."

Psalm 46:1-2

The dangers we face are often very real and dark. The situation, whether in the temporal or spiritual life, may appear to be utterly hopeless. There is always one hope: God's eye is on us. That eye sees the danger, sees in tender love His trembling and waiting child, set's the moment when the heart is ripe for the blessing, and sees the way in which it is to come.

The psalmist said, "The eye of the Loud is on those who fear Him, on those who hope in His mercy, to deliver their soul from death, and to keep them alive in famine" (33:18-19). He does not say the Lord will prevent the danger of death and famine—this is often needed to stir up people to wait on Him. He says the Lord will deliver and keep alive. He walks with us through hardships and heartaches.

Oh, the faithfulness of our God, who is a very present help in every time of trouble, a shield and defense against every danger. During the utmost spiritual famine, and when death appears to prevail, wait on God. He does deliver; He does keep alive.

Reflection

How quickly do you turn to God when difficult situations arise?

Why does He allow difficulties to enter our lives?

The Source of Living Water

"He who believes in Me, as the Scripture has
said, out of his heart will flow rivers of
living water."

John 7:38

Our Lord, during His conversation with the
Samaritan woman, said, "The water that I
shall give him will become in him a fountain
of water springing up into everlasting life" (John 4:14).
Later, Jesus used the imagery of water again and promised
that those who believe in Him will have rivers of living
water flowing from them, bringing life and blessing to
others.

What do we need in order to experience these two
wonderful promises of the well of water and the rivers
of living water? Just these things: the inner attachment
to Christ, the unreserved surrender to fellowship with
Him, and the firm assurance that His Spirit will work in
us what we cannot do. This is captured in Jesus' phrase,
"He who believes in Me" (John 7:38).

If the water from a reservoir is to flow into a house
all day, one thing is necessary—the connection must be
unobstructed and unhindered. Then the water passes
through the pipe of its own accord. So the union between
you and Christ must be uninterrupted; your faith must
accept Christ and depend on Him to sustain the new life.

Reflection

What kinds of
things interrupt the
connection between
you and Christ?

Why is belief vital
in keeping the living
water flowing?

God Longs for the Love of Your Heart

"The Lord your God will circumcise your
heart . . . to love the Lord your God with all
your heart and with all your soul."

Deuteronomy 30:6

God longs with a never-ending, fervent desire to have our love—the love of the whole heart. But how can we attain such a condition? In the same way that I receive salvation— through faith alone.

The apostle Paul says, "I live by faith in the Son of God, who loved me and gave Himself for me" (Gal. 2:20). When we take time to wait on God, and remember with what a burning desire God sought to win our love, we will realize that God has a strong and steadfast longing for the love of our hearts. Just as the sun is willing to give me its light and heat, if I will receive them, God is a thousand times more willing to give me the light and glow of His love.

In the Old Testament, God gave us the promise of the new covenant: "I will give you a new heart and put a new' spirit within you" (Ezek. 36:26). He gave His Son to die for us, in order to win our love. Take time to grasp this; wait silently on God, and become strong in the assurance of faith. God, who longs for your love, is almighty and will shed abroad His love in my heart through the Holy Spirit. God, who so greatly longs for your love, will work within you by His Spirit, will empower you to love Him with your whole heart and demonstrate your love by keeping His commandments.

Reflection

Why does God long for the love of your whole heart?

How are you responding to His call for your complete and absolute love?

Discover a Season of Quiet

"It is good that one should hope and wait
quietly for the salvation of the Lord."

Lamentations 3:26

Isaiah said that "quietness and confidence shall be your strength" (Isa. 30:15). Such words reveal to us the close connection between quietness and faith, and show us what a deep need there is for stillness and solitude. If we are to have our whole heart turned toward God, we must have it turned away from everything that distracts, disrupts, and diverts our attention from Him.

God is a being of such infinite greatness and glory, and our nature has become so estranged from Him, that it needs our whole heart and desires set up on Him. Everything that is not of God that excites our fears, stirs our efforts, awakens our hopes, or makes us glad hinders us in our perfect waiting on Him.

Take time to be separate from all clamor and duties, all cares and demands. Take time to be still and quiet before God. Take time not only to secure stillness from man and the world, but from self and its energy. Let your heart become calm and the Spirit hold back everything but God's whisper in your ear.

At first it may appear difficult to wait quietly and be still, with the activities of mind and heart subdued for a time. But the effort of pursuing it will be greatly rewarded. We will find that such discipline reaps a bounty of blessing. The season of silent worship will bring a kind of peace and rest that comes only from heaven.

Reflection

Which activities or thoughts keep you from being quiet before God?

Why arc many people uneasy during times of quiet?

When might you set aside time from your schedule to practice being still before God?

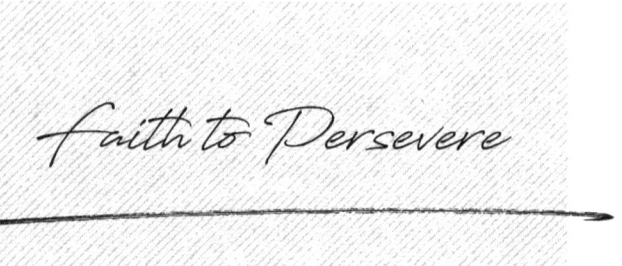

Faith to Persevere

"Fight the good fight of faith."

1 Timothy 6:12

Many Christians, when called on to persevere in prayer as intercessors, feel it is something entirely beyond their reach. They have not the power for the self-sacrifice and consecration necessary for such prayer. They shrink from the effort and struggle that will, they suppose, make them unhappy. They have tried, within their own power, to conquer the flesh—a wholly impossible thing. They have endeavored by Beelzebub to cast out Beelzebub, and this can never happen. Jesus alone can subdue the flesh and the devil.

The Scripture speaks of "the good fight of faith" (1 Tim. 6:12). That is to say, a fight springs from and is carried on by faith. We must attain an accurate understanding of faith and stand fast in our faith. Jesus Christ is always the "author and finisher" of faith (see Hebrews 12:2). When we come into right relationship with Him, we can be sure of the help and power He bestows.

In the first place, we must earnestly say, "Do not strive in your own strength; cast yourself at the feet of the Lord Jesus, and wait on Him in the sure confidence that He is with you and works in you." In the second place, we must say, "Strive in prayer; let faith fill your heart—so will you be strong in the Lord, and in the power of His might."

Faith in the love of Jesus is the only method of getting into fellowship with God in prayer.

Reflection

How much faith do you have in Jesus' love and His power to strengthen your prayer life? What might cause your faith to grow stronger and stronger?

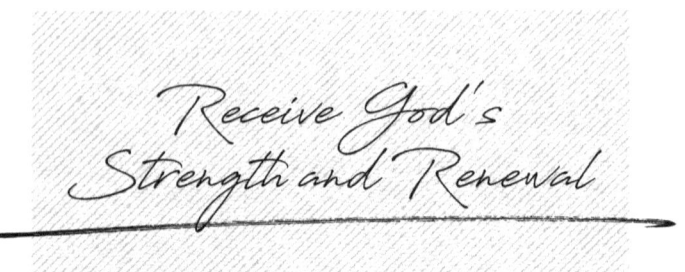

Receive God's Strength and Renewal

"Those who wait on the Lord shall renew their strength; they shall mount up with wings like eagles, they shall run and not be weary, they shall walk and not faint."

Isaiah 40:31

Believers are to live a heavenly life in the presence, love, and joy of God. They are to live where God lives. They need God's strength to rise there. To those who wait on Him, it will be given.

You know that eagles obtain their wings in only one way—through birth. You are born of God. You have the eagle's wings. You may not know it, you may not have used them, but God can and will teach you to use them.

Do you know how the eagles are taught the use of their wings? Look at the* cliff rising a thousand feet out of the sea. See the ledge high up on the rock where there is an eagle s nest with its treasure of two young eaglets. The mother bird stirs up her nest and with her beak nudges the timid birds over the precipice. Watch how they flutter, fall, and sink toward the depth. Then the mother flutters over her young, spreads out her wings, takes the eaglets up, and carries them on her wings. As they ride on her wings, she brings them to a place of safety. And she does this again and again.

God stirs your nest. He allows some hardship and

disappointment to come to you. He lets you fear and tremble, as all your strength fails and you feel utterly weary and helpless. All the while. He spreads His strong wings on which you can rest. And all He asks is that you sink down in your weariness, cling to Him, and allow Him in His Jehovah-strength to carry you as you ride on the wings of His omnipotence.

Reflection

In what ways is God "stirring up your nest"?

How are you responding?

In what situations are you most afraid to let God carry you?

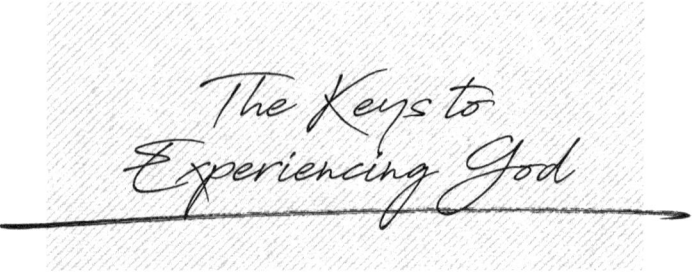

The Keys to Experiencing God

"Wait on the Lord, and keep His way, and He
shall emit you to inherit the land."

Psalm 37:34

W hen waiting on God, we need to lie careful that we keep His way. If we don't, we never can expect to find Him.

"Wait on the Loud" has to do with worship and disposition. "And keep His way" deals with our walk and work. The outer life must be in harmony with the inner; the inner must be the inspiration and strength for the outer. Our God has made known His way in His Word to guide our conduct. If we do not keep His w'ay, our waiting on Him can bring no blessing. Surrendering in full obedience to His will is the secret to the' blessings of His fellowship.

It is true that you don't yet have the strength to keep all of His way. But keep carefully those commands and instructions for which you have already received strength. Give up your whole being to God without reserve or doubt. He will prove Himself God to you and work in you that which is pleasing in His sight through Jesus Christ.

Reflection

Is your inner life in harmony with your outer life?

If not, what are you willing to do to correct the imbalance and, in trust, give yourself to God?

Looking back over your life so far, how has God demonstrated His faithfulness when you have "kept His way"?

Faith of the True Heart

"Therefore we also pray always for you that our God would count you worthy of this calling, and fulfill all the good pleasure of His goodness and the work of faith with power, that the name of our Lord Jesus Christ may be glorified in you."

2 Thessalonians 1:11–12

There is a faith of insight, a faith of desire, a faith of trust in the truth of the Word, and a faith of personal acceptance. There is a faith of love that embraces, a faith of will that holds fast, a faith of sacrifice that gives up everything, a faith of despair that abandons all hope in self, and a faith of rest that waits on God alone. This is all included in the faith of the true heart, in which the whole being surrenders and yields itself to God to do His work.

In fullness of faith, not of thought, let us draw near. What God is about to do to you is supernatural, above what you can think. God is the incomprehensible and hidden one. The Holy Spirit is the secret, unfathomable working and presence of God.

In fullness of faith, not in fullness of feeling, let us draw near. Look to God, who is able to do above what we ask or think. Look to Jesus on the throne, dwelling there to bring you in. Remember, these are all divine, spiritual mysteries of grace, to be revealed in you.

Reflection

Why do you think
Murray cautioned
about having
"fullness of
feeding"?

How does this differ
from "fullness of
faith"?

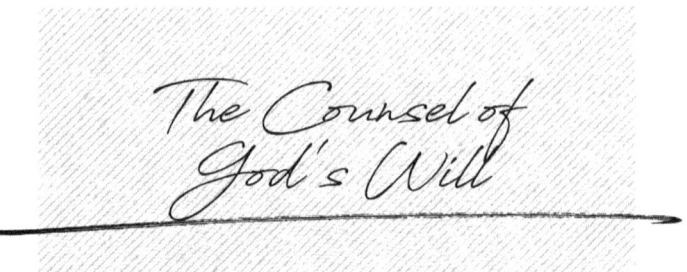

The Counsel of God's Will

"They soon forgot His works; they did not
wait for His counsel."

Psalm 106:13

Thuis was written about the sin of God's people in the wilderness. He had wonderfully re-deemed them and was prepared as wonderfully to supply their every need. But when the time of need came, "they did not wait for His counsel." They didn't think the almighty God was their leader and provider; they didn't ask what His plans might be. They simply clung to their own thoughts, and tempted and provoked God by their unbelief.

Our whole relation to God is ruled in this: His will is to be done in us and by us as it is in heaven. He has promised to make known His will to us by His Spirit, and our position is to wait for His counsel as the only guide for our thoughts and actions. During our church worship, prayer meetings, and gatherings, our first object ought always to be to ascertain the mind of God. He always works according to the counsel of His will. The more that counsel of His will is sought, found, and honored, the more surely and mightily God will do His work for us and through us.

The great danger in all assemblies is relying on our

own perceptions, past experiences, and utterances of wise people. These may indeed lead us in the right direction, but the truest and holiest guidance comes from God alone. God is eager to counsel and guide those who allow Him to have His way entirely, and who are willing to wait patiently for Him to make His will known.

Reflection

Spend time in prayer honoring God and patiently seeking His will.

Ask Him to show you any ways in which you are trusting in other things rather than seeking His will today.

Taking God's Word to Heart

"Trust in the Lord with all your heart, and
lean not on your own understanding."

Proverbs 3:5

S ome people suppose that if they are occupied
with the truth, their spiritual lives will as a
matter of course be strengthened. This is by
no means the case.

The understanding deals with conceptions and images
of divine things, but it cannot reach the real life of the
soul. Hence the command, "Trust in the Lord with all
your heart, and lean not on your own understanding."
With the heart, man believes and comes into touch with
God. In the heart, God has given His Spirit. It is the
heart that must trust, love, worship, and obey. My mind
is utterly impotent in creating or maintaining the spiritual life within me. The heart must wait on God for Him
to work it in me.

The Christian must always, when he has studied or
heard God's Word, cease from his thoughts and open up
his heart before God and seek living fellowship with Him.

Reflection

What's the
difference between
living fellowship
with God and
intellectual study of
biblical truths?

Share Love That Passes All Understanding

"A new commandment I give to you, that you love one another; as I have loved you, that you also love one another."

John 13:34

T he Lord gave His disciples a new commandment that they should love one another as He had loved them. To this end, He wanted them to know what the love was with which He had loved them. It is the everlasting, unchangeable, divine love with which the Father loved the Son, with which the Son loved us, and with which we should love one another. This thought is so vast and heavenly that it requires time for us to grasp it.

God sent His Son to earth to manifest this love. The same love that God had for His Son, He had in His heart for all mankind. Jesus exercised this same love toward His disciples. This same love was given to them when the Holy Spirit was poured out on the Day of Pentecost, that they might love one another and more—even love those who were enemies of Christ.

It is all one and the same love, not merely a feeling or a blessed experience, but a living divine power, flowing from the Father to the Son and working in the disciples' hearts through the Son, and so streaming forth to the whole world.

We are always ready to say, "We can't love others as Christ loved us." It is not impossible. The Holy Spirit, as the power of this love, pours it out in our hearts. This is God's own Word. He who meditates on it until he believes it will have the courage to bring his petitions to the throne of grace and receive the love that passes all understanding.

Reflection

Pray and ask God's Spirit to make this kind of love a reality in your life.
Thank Him for His deep love for you.

The Secret of True Godliness

"The Lord is near to all who call upon Him,
to all who call upon Him in truth."

Psalm 145:18

D o you long to experience continually the nearness of God? Here is the secret: "Pray without ceasing." Then you will have this assurance: "The Lord is near to all who call upon Him." Prayer has a wonderful power of helping us draw near to God and keeping us in His presence. God is always ready and able to grant us unbroken fellowship with Him.

Want to know the secret of always abiding in a state of prayerfulness? The answer is clear. First, realize that God is near you and within you, and then you will feel how natural it is to talk with Him every moment about your needs and desires. This is the secret of the prayerful life of which Paul writes: "night and day praying exceedingly" (1 Thess. 3:10).

It is only when you live a life apart from God that you say, "I must take time. I must take trouble first of all to find God before I can pray." But to the true Christian, life is a constant abiding with the Father. "In Your name they rejoice all day long" (Ps. 89:16). The communion between the Father and His child should be continuous. Then prayer may become a moment-by- moment activity, like breathing, instead of something that is done only once a daw The principle of complete dependence on the unseen God. and the holy habit of claiming His presence with us each moment of the day—this is the secret of a life of true godliness.

Reflection

What has this reading revealed about prayer—and your prayerfulness?

How would life be different if you were continually dependent on and in communication with God?

Giving Ourselves to God

"You shall love the Lord your God with all your heart, with all your soul, with all your mind, and with all your strength."

Mark 12:30

In this great command, the Lord our God has tried to teach us how greatly He wants us wholly for Himself. Our love, prayers, consecration, trust, obedience—in all these, there must be an unreserved surrender to God's will and service.

"With all your heart"—with its longings, affections, attachments, all its desires. "With all your soul"—until its vital powers and the will as a royal master in the soul. "With all your mind"—with its faculties of thought, knowledge, reasoning, memory, and imagination. "With all your strength"—with complete energy and exertion given over to God's purposes.

What a wonderful God it is who has such a right to expect so much from us! Is He not the perfect and glorious one, who is so worthy that we should forsake all to follow Him? Is He not the everlasting love and goodness and mercy, always desirous of pouring out blessings on us? Is He not so deserving of praise that we ought to love and honor Him with all our strength and all our heart? Take this commandment into your heart, make it the rule of your life, and try to realize that God must have all of you.

Reflection

Praise God for all
that He has done for
you.
Ask Him to teach
you what this type
of love for Him is
all about.

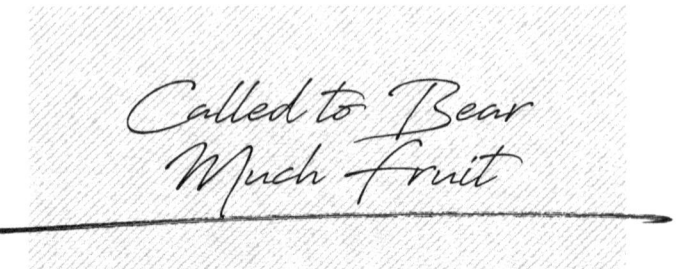

Called to Bear Much Fruit

"I am the vine, you are the branches. He who
abides in Me, and I in him, bears much fruit .
. . By this My Father is glorified, that you
bear much fruit; so you will be My disciples."

John 15:5,8

A tree or vine yields fruit for the benefit of its
owner. We, as branches of the heavenly Vine,
receive and enjoy such astounding grace so
we may win souls for Him.

Could this be the reason why you have not enjoyed
unbroken fellowship with Christ? Perhaps you have
forgotten that the object of fellowship and communion
is fruit-bearing in saving other people. Haven't you given
too much thought to your own sanctification and joy, not
remembering that as Christ sought His blessing and
glory from the Father in the sacrifice of Himself for us,
so we, too, are called to live solely to bring Christ to
others? For this purpose, we become branches of the
heavenly Vine, in order to continue the work He began.

When Christ was on earth, He said, "I am the light
of the world" (John 8:12). But speaking of the time when
He would be taken from the earth. He said, "You are the
light of the world" (Matt. 5:14).

How often you have said to the Lord, "I yield myself
to you for cleansing and keeping and to be made holy,"

but you have hesitated to add, "to be used by you for the salvation of others." Let us acknowledge our reluctance and humbly offer ourselves to the Lord for His work. Let us begin by praying for people around us, seeking opportunities to help them, refusing to be satisfied until we bear fruit to the glory of the Father.

Reflection

Ask God to increase your desire to share Him with other people and to guide you in building sincere relationships with people who don't yet know Him.

Trust Him to use you to reflect His light, and begin praying for specific people.

The Three Activities of the Soul

"Whatever things you ask when you pray,
believe that you receive them, and you will
have them."

Mark 11:24

To know, to desire, to will—these are the three
chief activities of the soul. When a Christian
realizes the fullness there is in Christ and the
abundant life He gives, these three words will show him
the way to participate in this fullness.

To know: We must not be content with our own
thoughts about growth in grace. We must see to it that
we know clearly what God promises to do in us and what
He requires of us. God's Word teaches us that if we
honestly and sincerely yield to Christ our Lord, He will
do in us far above what we dare think.

To desire: We must be careful to desire with our whole
heart that for which we pray—and be willing to pay the
price for it. Perhaps our desire is weak. God will create
the desire in answer to prayer. It may cost us a struggle,
and much self-sacrifice, to let go of the world and self.
But the Spirit will come to our aid, for without strong
desire and self-sacrifice, progress will not be made.

To will: Only with resolute faith will you have
courage to appropriate what God bestows. Often in the

midst of fear and struggle, we will to grasp what God offers. Our confidence must be in God alone. When our desire has developed into a firm will, we will have courage to believe all that God has promised.

Reflection

Meditate on what God promises to do in you.

Ask God to increase your desire as you pray and to give you the faith to believe His promises.

Jesus is Working in You

"He who abides in Me, and I in him, bears much fruit; for without Me you can do nothing."

John 15:5

Jesus follows up His great promise that those who abide in Him will bear much fruit with the words "without Me you can do nothing."

What a cause for humility! Because the nature we inherit from Adam is so corrupt, no good thing lives in us—that is, in our flesh. In fact, our flesh is antagonistic toward God. We are under sin's power to such an extent that we cannot do anything well pleasing to God.

What a call to repentance! How often we Christians have thought that we were able to do that which is good. How often we thought we were making ourselves better. Let's remember that without Him we can do nothing, and henceforth rely only on Him.

What a reason for thanksgiving! Christ has united us to Himself, and so lives in us. He may work in and through us each day and all day. This is the secret of the spiritual life: Jesus working in us, enabling us to do His work.

What a reason for joy and encouragement! I have to care about one thing only—that I remain utterly dependent on Him to care for me and work through me each day. Whenever I remember that without Christ I can do nothing, I also remember, "He who abides in Me . . . bears much fruit."

Reflection

Why can't we, on our own, do anything that pleases God?

What does it mean to be utterly dependent on God?

What may God enable you to do today?

The Cause of Prayerlessness

"Those who are Christ's have crucified the
flesh with its passions and desires."

Galatians 5:24

I t is discouraging to consider how many Christians seldom think or speak earnestly about the
deep and immeasurable sinfulness of "the flesh."
As Paul said, "In me (that is, in my flesh) nothing good
dwells" (Rom. 7:18). The man who truly believes this
may well cry out, "O wretched man that I am! Who will
deliver me from this body of death?" (Rom. 7:24).

The deep root of sin is the cause of a prayerless life.
The flesh can say prayers well enough, calling itself
religious for so doing and thus satisfying conscience. But
the flesh has no desire or strength for the prayer that
strives after an intimate knowledge of God, rejoices in
fellowship with Him, and continues to lay hold of His
strength. So, finally, it comes to this: The flesh must be
denied and crucified.

The Christian who is bound by fleshly desires and
attitudes has neither disposition nor strength to follow
after God. He rests satisfied with the prayer of habit or
custom—but the blessedness of intimate, secret prayer
is a hidden thing to him. He will gain the full measure
of blessing only when his eyes are opened and he begins

to see that the flesh, in its disposition to turn away from God, is the archenemy that makes powerful prayer impossible for him.

Reflection

Take time to think about your prayer life and the excuses you may be making for not praying. What causes prayerlessness in your life?

Heavenly Mindedness

"We have received, not the spirit of the world, but the Spirit who is from God, that we might know the things that have been freely given to us by God."

1 Corinthians 2:12

Christ taught us to think of God as our heavenly Father, who is ready to bestow His blessings on His children on earth. The Holy Spirit comes to us to pour into our hearts all the light, love, joy, and power of heaven.

Those who are truly filled with the Spirit have a heavenly life in themselves. Their walk and conversation are filled with the attributes of heaven. They are in daily fellowship with the Father and the Son. They seek the things that are above, and their chief characteristic is heavenly mindedness.

How can one cultivate this heavenly disposition? By allowing the Holy Spirit to do His heavenly work in our hearts and to bring to ripeness in our souls the fruits of the Spirit that grow in the Paradise of God. The Spirit will raise our hearts daily to fellowship with God in heaven and will teach us to dwell in the heavenlies with Him. The Spirit makes the glorified Christ in heaven present in our hearts and teaches us to live in His abiding presence.

Reflection

Take time today to invite the Holy Spirit to work in your heart and mind, to strengthen you—a child of heaven—during your spiritual journey here on earth.

Believe that God wants to give you His blessings.

Living in God's Presence

"Lead me in Your truth and teach me, for You are the God of my salvation; on You I wait all the day."

Psalm 25:5

It is a step forward in the Christian life when one decides to seek to have fellowship with God in His Word each day without fail. His perseverance will be crowned with success, if he is really in earnest.

On waking in the morning, God will be his first thought. He must set aside time for prayer and resolve to give God time to hear his requests and reveal himself to him. Then he may speak out all his desires to God and expect an answer. Later on in the day, even if only for a few minutes, he will take time to keep up the fellowship with God. And again in the evening, a quiet period is necessary to review the day's work and with confession of sin receive the assurance of forgiveness.

Such a person will gradually gain insight into what is lacking in his life. He will realize that the Holy Spirit is in him unceasingly, just as his breathing is continuous. He will make it his aim to gain the assurance through faith that the Holy Spirit, Jesus, and the Father will grant His presence and help all through the day.

Reflection

Why is fellowship
with God in His
Word vital as we
seek to know Him
better and allow His
presence to
permeate
everything we do?

Understanding Divine Truth

"That the God of our Lord Jesus Christ, the
Father of glory, may give to you the spirit of
wisdom and revelation in the knowledge of
Him, the eyes of your understanding being
enlightened."

Ephesians 1:17–18

I n the Word of God, we find a wonderful combination of the human and the divine. The language is that of a man. Anyone who has a good understanding can grasp the meaning of the words and the truths contained in them. Yet this is all that man, in the power of his human understanding, can do.

There is a divine side in which God expresses His deepest thoughts to us. The carnal person cannot attain to them, or comprehend them, because they must be "spiritually discerned." Only through the Holy Spirit can the Christian understand the divine truth contained in God's Word. Paul prays earnestly that God would grant the spirit of wisdom to his readers, eyes that are enlightened through the Holy Spirit to understand what is written and know the exceeding greatness of His power working in all who believe.

Paul teaches us that when we read God's Word, or meditate on it, we should pray, "Father, grant me the spirit of wisdom and revelation." As we do this each day, we will find that God's Word is living and powerful.

God's commands will be changed into promises. His commands are not grievous. The Holy Spirit will teach us to do, lovingly and joyfully, all that He has commanded.

Reflection

Why do some people fail to fully grasp the deep truths found in God's Word?

Pray that God will reveal His Spirit of wisdom and truth to you as you read and meditate on His Word.

The Lessons of the Seed

"A sower went out to sow his seed . . . The seed is the word of God."

Luke 8:5,11

T he seed teaches us most precious lessons concerning our use of God's Word. There is first the Lesson of Faith. Faith doesn't look at appearances. As far as we can judge, it looks most improbable that a Word of God should give life in the soul, work in us the very grace of which it speaks, transform our whole character, and fill us with strength. And so it is.

Then there is the Lesson of Labor. The seed needs to be gathered, kept, and put into prepared soil. Likewise, the mind has to gather from Scripture and pass on to the heart, as the only soil in which this heavenly seed can grow.

The seed teaches the Lesson of Patience. The Word's effect on the heart is in most cases not immediate. It needs time to strike root and grow up. Christ's words must abide in us. We must not only day by day increase our store of Bible knowledge—this is only like gathering grain in a barn—but watch over those words that we have received. We must allow then room in our heart to spread roots and branches.

Last comes the Lesson of Fruitfulness. However insignificant that little seed of a Word of God appears, the fruit will surely come. The truth, life, and power of God will grow and ripen within you. And just as a seed bears a fruit, containing the same seed for new' reproduction, so the Word will bring you not only fruit, but also a seed you can carry to others to give life and blessing.

Reflection

Are there obstacles that keep you from fully receiving the Bible's wisdom and power in your life?

Think about how you can apply each of the lessons mentioned above to your knowledge and understanding of the Bible.

Serving in Prayer

"Brethren, pray for us."

1 Thessalonians 5:25

Intercession is an indispensable part of prayer. It strengthens our love and faith in what God can do and is a means of bringing blessing and salvation to others. Let us learn this lesson thoroughly: Prayer should not be for ourselves alone, but chiefly for other people. Let us begin by praying for those who are near and dear to us —those with whom we live. Pray for divine wisdom, thoughtfulness, kindness, and self-sacrifice on their behalf.

Pray for all your friends and all with whom you come into contact. Pray that you may watch in prayer for their souls. Pray for all Christians, especially for ministers and those in responsible positions.

Pray for those who do not yet know the Lord as their Savior. Make a list of the names of those whom God has laid on your heart, and pray for their conversion. You belong to Christ; He needs you to bring to Him in prayer the souls of those around you. Do you think this will take too much time? Just think what an inconceivable blessing it is to help people through your prayers, and look to the Holy Spirit for further guidance. Cultivate the conviction, "I am saved to serve."

Reflection

Why is praying for other people so important?

Which people will you begin praying for today?

Faith Working through Love

"For in Christ Jesus neither circumcision nor
uncircumcision avails anything, but faith
working through love."

Galatians 5:6

F aith is the root; love is the fruit. Faith becomes
strong in the love of God and of Christ. Faith
in God and showing love to the brethren must
always go hand in hand. Faith in God's wonderful love,
permeating our hearts, enables us to live always in love
toward our fellow men. This true faith gives us power
for a life of fervent, all-embracing love.

All of our lives should be spent exhibiting the love
of Christ. O Christian, the whole of salvation lies in
these two words—faith and love. Let our faith cling to
God's Word and to the miraculous things He will do for
us each day. Let these thoughts about love impel us to
accept with new and greater faith the love of God. Let
our faith each day take deeper root in Gods eternal love.
Then each day the fruit of the Spirit will be love in all
our interactions with those around us.

Reflection

What's the relationship between faith in God and loving other people?

Which people might God want you to love with His love during the coming week—including someone who seems to be unlovable?

God's Word: the Power of the Divine Life

"The word of God is living and powerful."

Hebrews 4:12

I find it a great help to use much of God's Word in my prayers. If the Holy Spirit impresses a certain text on my mind, I take it to the throne of grace and plead the promise. This habit increases our faith, reminds us of God's promises, and brings us into harmony with His will. We learn to pray according to God's will and understand that we can only expect an answer when our prayers are in accordance with that will (see 1 John 5:14).

Prayer is like fire. Fire can only burn brightly if it is supplied with good fuel. That fuel is God's Word, which must not only be studied carefully and prayerfully, but must also be taken into the heart and lived out in the life. The inspiration and powerful workings of the Holy Spirit alone can do this. By thoughts such as these, we gain deeper insight into the value and power of God's Word as the fuel, energy, and fervor of our spiritual lives.

Reflection

How might you use
God's Word as you
pray, if you aren't
already doing so?

What do you think
it means to "plead
the promise" during
prayer?

Living in the Spirit

"But you, beloved, building yourselves up on
your most holy faith, praying in the Holy
Spirit, keep yourselves in the love of God."

Jude 20-21

Just as the Christian needs to be strong in the Lord all the day, and to wear his armor against the foe the whole day, so needs to live always praying in the Spirit. The Holy Spirit will not come to us, nor work within us, only at certain times when we think we need His aid. The Spirit comes to be our life companion. He wants us wholly in His possession at all times; otherwise He cannot do His work in us.

Many Christians do not understand this. They want the Spirit to help them and empower them when the need arises, but do not understand that He must dwell in them continually and have full possession of their entire being. Once this truth is grasped, we will realize that it is possible to live always "praying . . . in the Spirit." By faith we may have the assurance that the Spirit will keep us in a prayerful attitude so we might enjoy continual fellowship with God.

Reflection

Why do some
people invite the
Holy Spirit's
presence only at
certain times?

How can you better
allow the Spirit to
be your continual
life companion?

God's Will in You

"Understand what the will of the Lord is."

Ephesians 5:17

To live a life in dependence on the Father and conformity to His Son, the first thing that is necessary is a firm belief that He will make known His will to us. This keeps many back. They cannot believe that the Lord cares for them so much that He will indeed give Himself the trouble every day to teach them and make known to them His will, just as He did to Jesus.

Christian, you are more valuable to the Father than you know. You are as valuable as the price He paid for you—that is, the blood of His Son. He therefore attaches the highest value to the least thing that concerns you and will guide you even in what is most insignificant. He longs more for close and constant communication with you than you can conceive. He can use you for His glory and make something of you, higher than you can understand.

If up to this point you have know'll but little of this life of conscious dependence and simple obedience, begin today. Let your Savior be your example in this. It is His blessed will to live in you, and in you to be again what He was here on earth.

Reflection

How valuable do you really believe you are to the Father?

If you believe that God cares about every aspect of your life, how might that affect your dependence on Him and your willingness to pursue His will for your life?

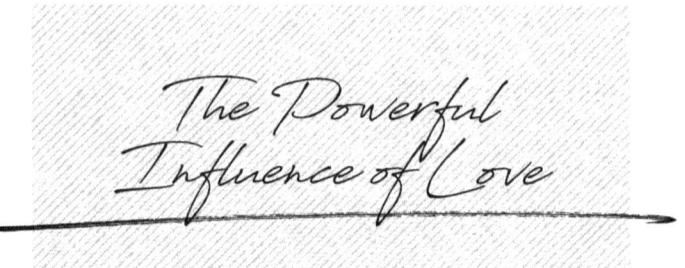

The Powerful Influence of Love

"Let all that you do be done with love."

1 Corinthians 16:14

During days of unrest, we need above all a new discovery— and living experience—of the love of God. God's power, by which He rules and guides the world, is the power of an undying, persistent love. He works through the hearts, spirits, and walls of men and women who are completely yielded to Him and His service. He waits for them to open their hearts to Him in love, and then, full of courage, to become witnesses for Him.

The only means Christ used to gain influence was through the manifestation of a great, serving, suffering love. He saw the possibility of redemption in the hearts of even the worst of men. He knew that men's hearts could never resist the steady, continuous influence of love, and that unbounded faith in God's love would be our strength and anchor. In the fire and fervor of that love, the disciples were able to expect, and to do, the impossible.

The spirit of hatred and bitterness can never be overcome by argument or reproaches. God's children must learn to accept His love, not only for themselves individually but also for the lives of others.

Reflection

How are you influencing others by demonstrating God's love?

How might you respond in love the next time you face hatred or bitterness?

The Sign of a True Church

"The love of God has been poured out in our
hearts by the Holy Spirit who was given to
us."

Romans 5:5

I n God, love reaches its highest point and is the
culmination of His glory. In the man Christ Jesus
on the cross, love is at its highest. We owe everything to this love. Love is the power that moved Christ
to die for us. Love is the power through which Christ
dwells in us and works in us. Every Christian should
show forth, as a mirror, the love of God.

Alas, how seldom do Christians realize this! They
seek, in the power of human love, to love Christ and the
brethren. And then they fail. They are sure it is impossible
to lead such a life, and they do not even greatly desire it
or pray for it. They don't understand that we can love,
with Gods own love, which is poured forth into our hearts
by the Holy Spirit.

If we fully believe that the Holy Spirit, dwelling
within us, will maintain this heavenly love from hour to
hour, we will be able to understand the word of Christ:
"All things are possible to him who believes" (Mark 9:23).

Reflection

What are some
different
characteristics
between human love
and God's love?

How effective is the
church today at
loving unbelievers?

Faith in Daily Life

"As you therefore have received Christ Jesus
the Lord, so walk in Him, rooted and built up
in Him and established in the faith."

Colossians 2:6

In these words, the apostle teaches us the weighty lesson that it is not only by faith that we first come to Christ and are united to Him, but that it is by faith that we are to be rooted and established in our union with Christ.

There are earnest Christians who do not understand this or, if they admit it in theory, fail to realize its application in practice. They are very zealous about the free gift of salvation, with our first acceptance of Christ and justification by faith alone. But after this, they think everything depends on our diligence and faithfulness. Although they firmly grasp the truth that the sinner will be justified by faith, they have hardly found a place in their scheme for the larger truth, "The just shall live by faith" (Rom. 1:17). They have never understood what a perfect Savior Jesus is. They don't know that the life of grace is always and only a life of faith, and that in the relationship to Jesus, the one daily and unceasing duty of the disciple is to believe, because believing is the one channel through which divine grace and strength flow out into the heart of man.

Reflection

What is involved in living by faith?

What is the relationship between faith and belief?

Abide in the Vine

"I am the true vine . . . Abide in Me."

John 15:1, 4

Oh, that you would learn a lesson from the time when you first came to the Savior! Remember, dear soul, how you then were led to take Jesus at His word and how you were not disappointed. He did receive you and pardon you. He did love you and save you. And if He did this for you when you were an enemy and stranger, now that you are His own, will He not much more fulfill His promise?

By His almighty grace, you are already in Him. By faith, you become partakers of the initial grace; by that same faith, you can enjoy the continuous grace of abiding in Him. If you ask what exactly you now have to believe in order to abide in Him, the answer is not difficult. Believe first of all what He says: "I am the Vine." The safety and fruitfulness of the branch depend on the vine's strength.

Don't think so much about yourself as a branch, nor about your duty to abide, until your soul has been filled with the faith of what Christ as the Vine is. He really will be to you all that a vine can be—holding you securely, nourishing you, supplying all you need for growth. Take time to know and heartily believe this: My Vine, on whom we can depend for all we need, is Christ.

Reflection

In what specific ways does Jesus, the Vine, nourish you?

How might you better tap into His resources to grow and flourish even more?

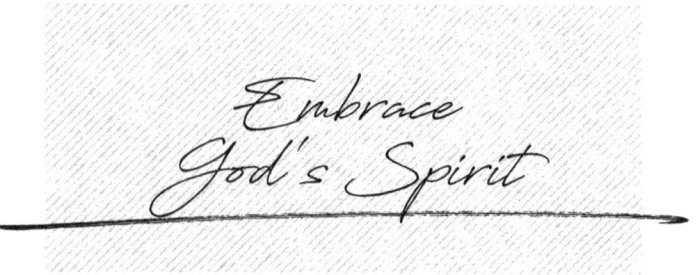

Embrace God's Spirit

"You will seek Me and find Me, when you
search for Me with all your heart."

Jeremiah 29:13

Y ou have often heard it said that if one seeks
to perform any great work, he must do it with
his whole heart and with all his powers. In
worldly matters, this is the secret of success and victory.
And it is indispensable in divine things, especially in
praying for the Holy Spirit.

I cannot too earnestly or urgently state that the Holy
Spirit desires to possess you fully. He can be satisfied
with nothing less if He is to show His full power in your
life. He has the right. Why? Because He is the Almighty
God.

Have you realized that when you pray for the Holy
Spirit you are praying for the whole Godhead to take
possession of you? Or were you expecting that God
would do something in your heart, but for the rest you
have to be free to do your own will? The Holy Spirit
must have full possession.

God has ordained in His divine providence that the
Holy Spirit will work within you to do all you need. What
God commands and demands of us. He will Himself

work within us. On our part, we must earnestly pray to the Father each day and accept the Holy Spirit as our leader and guide.

Reflection

Do you desire that the Holy Spirit possess you fully? Why or why not?

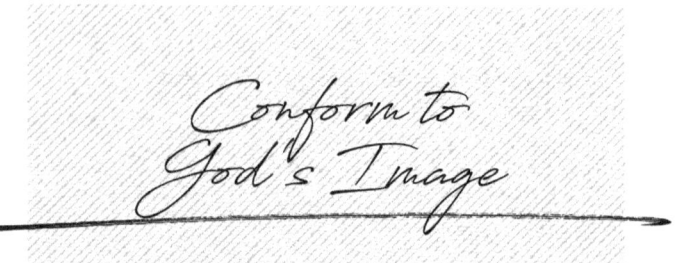

Conform to God's Image

"Let us run with endurance the race that is set before us, looking unto Jesus, the author and finisher of our faith, who for the joy that was set before Him endured the cross, despising the shame."

Hebrews 12:1-2

In running a race, the athlete's eyes and heart are always set on the goal and prize. Here, the Christian is called to keep his eye fixed on Jesus enduring the cross, as the one object of imitation and desire.

The impotence of the church is greatly due to the f act that this cross-bearing mind of Jesus is so little preached and practiced. Most Christians think that as long as they don't commit actual sin, they are at liberty to possess and enjoy as much of the world as they please. There is so little insight into the deep truth that the world, and the flesh that loves the world, is enmity against God. Consequently, main Christians seek and pray for years for conformity to the image of Jesus, yet fail so entirely. They do not seek with the whole heart to know what it is to die to self and the world.

It was for the joy set before Him that Christ endured the cross—the joy of pleasing and glorifying the Father. Through His endurance of the cross, only in our fellowship of the cross, can we really become conformed to the image of God's Son.

Reflection

What do you think it means to die to self and the world?

How much do you want to be conformed to the image of God's Son?

Feed on the Word

> "Man shall not live by bread alone, but by every word that proceeds from the mouth of God."

Matthew 4:4

Bread is indispensable to life. However strong a person may be, if he takes no nourishment, he will grow weak and eventually die.

Bread must be eaten. I may have bread in my house and on my table in great abundance—but if I cannot or will not eat it, I'll die. Likewise, mere knowledge of God's Word will not help me. It is not enough to hold it and think about it; I must feed on God's Word. As it is absorbed into my life, I am sustained and strengthened.

Bread must be eaten daily. The same is true of God's Word. The psalmist says, "Blessed is the man [whose] delight is in the law of the Lord, and in His law he meditates day and night" (Ps. 1:1-2). To secure a strong and powerful spiritual life, feeding on God's Word every day is indispensable.

When on earth, the Lord Jesus learned, loved, and obeyed the Father's Word. And if you seek fellowship with Him, you will find Him in His Word.

Reflection

How greatly do you desire the powerful Word of God?

Do you delight in it?

What happens to a Christian who neglects the Bible or has only a superficial knowledge of it?

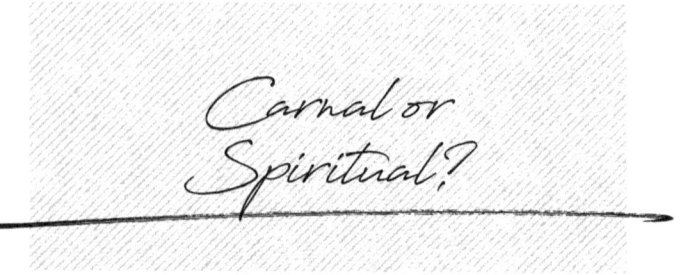

Carnal or
Spiritual?

"And I, brethren, could not speak to you as to
spiritual people but as to carnal, as to babes
in Christ."

1 Corinthians 3:1

The Christian who walks in the Spirit and has crucified the flesh is spiritual (see Gal. 5:24). The Christian who walks after the flesh and wishes to please the flesh is carnal (see Rom. 13:14).

What a difference there is between the carnal and the spiritual Christian! With the carnal Christian, there may be much religion and much zeal for God—but it is for the most part in human power. With the spiritual, on the other hand, there is a complete subjection to the Spirit's leading, a deep sense of weakness and entire dependence on the work of Christ.

How important it is for us to find out and plainly acknowledge before God whether we are spiritual or carnal! What a change is necessary for a Christian who is chiefly carnal to become truly spiritual. At first he cannot understand what must happen, or how it can come to pass. The more the truth dawns on him, the more he is convinced that it is impossible unless God does it.

Reflection

What's the difference between the carnal and the spiritual Christian?

Why does a carnal Christian who wants to become truly spiritual need to spend time in prayer?

Confidence in Christ

"You are in Christ Jesus, who became for us
wisdom from God."

1 Corinthians 1:30

All that you can wish to know is perfectly clear to Christ. As man, as mediator, He has access to the counsels of deity, to the secrets of providence, in your interest and on your behalf. If you will but trust Him fully, and abide in Him entirely, you can be confident ol receiving unerring guidance.

Seek to maintain the spirit of waiting and dependence, which always seeks to learn and will not move until the heavenly light leads on. Surrender all of your own wisdom. Seek a deep conviction of the utter blindness of the natural understanding in the things of God. Wait for Jesus to teach and guide in what you have to believe and have to do.

Meet frequently with Him in the inner chamber ol the heart, where the Spirit's gentle voice is only heard if all is still. Hold fast with unshaken confidence, even during the midst of darkness and apparent desertion. Live, above all, day by day in the blessed truth that, because the living Christ Jesus is your wisdom, your first and last care must always be this alone—to abide in Him.

Reflection

How has God's wisdom been demonstrated in your life?

What are you doing to abide in Him, to demonstrate trust in His guidance and sensitivity to His teaching?

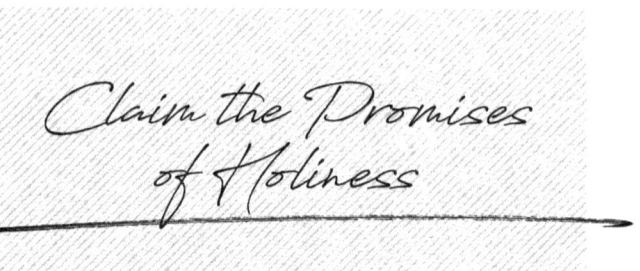

Claim the Promises of Holiness

"As He who called you is holy, you also be
holy in all your conduct."

1 Peter 1:15

There is no other way we can become holy but by becoming partakers of Christ's holiness. And there is no other way this can take place than by our spiritual union with Him so that, through His Spirit, His holy life flows into us.

Don't be afraid to claim God's promises to make you holy. Don't listen to the suggestion that the corruption of your old nature makes holiness impossible. It is true that no good thing dwells in your flesh, but the pure Spirit of God now dwells within you as well. That holy life is mightier than your evil life, and that new life can keep down the workings of the evil life within you.

Remember, this holy nature in you is singularly fitted for living a holy life and performing all holy duties, just as the old nature is fitted for doing evil. Understand that this holy nature in you has its root and life in Christ in heaven. Above all, believe confidently that Jesus delights in maintaining that new nature within you and imparting to it His strength and wisdom for its work.

Reflection

What exactly does holiness mean to you?

Why is it so important in a believer's life?

How can you know for sure that God will make you holy and subdue your sinful nature?

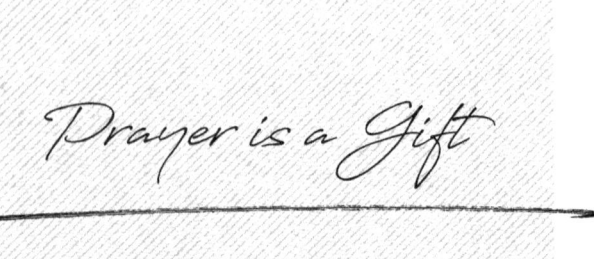
Prayer is a Gift

"The Lord . . . wondered that there was no intercessor."

Isaiah 59:15–16

Christ became man so that, both on earth and in heaven, He might intercede for all of mankind. And before He left the world, He imparted this right of intercession to His disciples, that whatever they should ask for, He would do for them (see John 15-17).

God's intense longing to bless seems in some sense to be graciously limited by His dependence on the intercession that rises from the earth. He seeks to rouse the spirit of intercession so that He may be able to bestow His blessing on those who seek Him. God regards intercession as the highest expression of His people's readiness to receive and to yield themselves completely to the working of His almighty power.

Christians need to realize this as their true nobility and their only power with God—the right to claim and expect that God will hear prayer. It is only as God's children begin to see what intercession means in regard to God's kingdom that they will realize how solemn their responsibility is. Intercession in its omnipotent power is according to God's will and is most certainly effectual!

Reflection

Why do some
Christians view
prayer as an
obligation to
perform rather than
a gift to enjoy?

What do you think
is the relationship
between
intercession and
God's blessings?

Will you Testify About Jesus?

"You shall be witnesses to Me in Jerusalem,
and in all Judea and Samaria, and to the end
of the earth."

Acts 1:8

Christ's servants are to be witnesses to Him, always testifying of His wonderful love, His power to redeem, and His wonderful power to work in them. Without claiming authority or power, without wisdom or eloquence, each one is called to be a living proof and witness of what Jesus can do. This is what the first disciples did. When they were filled with the Spirit, they began to speak of the mighty things Christ had done.

In this power, those who were scattered abroad by persecution went forth preaching in Jesus' name, so that a multitude of people believed. They had no commission from the apostles, no special gifts or training. But out of the fullness of their hearts, they spoke of Jesus Christ. They could not be silent. They were filled with Christs life and love and could not help but witness for Him.

Here we have the secret of a flourishing church: every believer being a witness for Jesus. Here we have the cause of the church's weakness: so few who are willing in daily life to testify that Jesus is Lord.

Reflection

With whom are you sharing Jesus—someone at work, in your neighborhood, in your social group?

If you are reluctant to tell others what Jesus has done for you, why is this?

Our Holy Calling

"Paul, a bondservant of Jesus Christ."

Romans 1:1

L et us accept distinctly and joyfully our holy calling, that we are even now to live as the servants of the love of Jesus to our fellow men. We must live so that some of the holiness and gentleness of Christ may shine out in us. We must live to represent Him, as was the case with Him when on earth.

What the church and the world both need is this: men and women seized by the Holy Spirit and compelled by love, men and women who are living embodiments of the grace and power of Christ. With hearts longing to have Jesus glorified, let us offer ourselves in service to Him. There is work among the sick, the poor, and the outcast. There is work in a hundred different paths that the Spirit of Christ opens up to us. There is work for us in ways that have not yet been opened up by others.

Let us work, not like those who do so to gain approval and applause from others. No, let us work as those who are growing more like Christ and who, like Him, consider Kingdom work to be the very joy and glory of heaven begun on earth.

Reflection

What work may the Spirit of Christ be opening up for you?

How might you share Jesus' love with people in your circles of influence?

Why is it important to show His love and not just talk about it?

Taking Up the Cross of Christ

"God forbid that I should boast except in the cross of our Lord Jesus Christ, by whom the world has been crucified to me, and I to the world."

Galatians 6:14

We must learn to look on the cross as not only an atonement to God, but also a victory over the devil. The cross means not only deliverance from the guilt, but also from the power of sin. Christs death opens the way for close union and fellowship with Him, as we partake of His full power over sin and the new life of victory.

Some Christians are content to look on the cross as the place Christ died for their sins, but they have little heart for fellowship with the crucified one. Or they are content to consider the ordinary afflictions of life, which the children of the world often have as much as they, as their share of Christ's cross. They have no conception of what it is to be crucified with Christ, that bearing the cross means likeness to Christ in the principles that animated Him in His path of obedience.

The surrender of all self-will, the complete denial of fleshly desires, the separation from the world in all its ways of thinking and acting, the sacrifice of self for the sake of others—these are the marks of the person who has taken up Christ's cross. These are characteristics of those who seek to say, "I am crucified with Christ; I abide in Christ, the crucified one.

Reflection

What victory did Jesus' death on the cross accomplish?

Think about what it means to completely deny the desires and pleasures of the flesh.

How can we walk Jesus' path of obedience and be victorious over the sinful world's ways of thinking and acting?

Wait on God in Prayer

"Be still, and know that I am God; I will be
exalted among the nations, I will be exalted
in the earth!"

Psalm 46:10

I f an army is given orders to march into an enemy's country and yet does not immediately
advance, the question will be asked, "What is
causing the delay?" The answer will often be, "Waiting
for supplies." All the supplies of provisions, clothing, or
ammunition have not arrived. Without these, the army
dare not proceed.

It is the same in the Christian life. Day by day, we
need our supplies from above. There is nothing we need
more than to cultivate that spirit of dependence on God
and of confidence in Him, which refuses to go on without
the needed supply of grace and strength.

If someone asks whether this is different from what
we do when we pray, the answer is that there may be
much petitioning but little waiting on God. When we
pray, we are often occupied with ourselves, our needs,
and our efforts in presenting them.

In waiting on God, the first thought is of the God
on whom we wait. We enter His presence and feel we
need to be quiet so that He, as God, can overshadow us

with Himself. God longs to reveal Himself and fill us with Himself. Waiting on God gives Him time in His own wav and divine power to come to us.

Before you pray, bow quietly before God just to remember and realize who He is, how near He is, how certainly He can help. Be still before Him and allow His Holy Spirit to waken and stir up in your soul the childlike disposition of absolute dependence and confident expectation. Wait on God until you know you have met Him. Prayer will then become so different.

Reflection

When you pray, do you quietly focus on Him first—on who He is, how near He is?

Do you allow the Holy Spirit to fill you with a sense of dependence and confident expectation?

A Living Fellowship

"My voice You shall hear in the morning, O Lord; in the morning I will direct it to You, and I will look up."

Psalm 5:3

E ven the most sincere and committed Christian faces a danger: it is the danger of substituting prayer and Bible study for living fellowship with God. Your desire to pray earnestly and diligently may so occupy you that the light of His countenance and the joy of His love cannot enter you. Your Bible study may so interest you and intrigue you that, yes, the very Word of God may become a substitute for God Himself. These pursuits can hinder fellowship because they keep the mind, heart, and soul occupied instead of leading you into the presence of God.

What a difference it would make if everything were subordinate to this one aim: All through the day, I will walk with God—I shall be with Him moment by moment as a child is with his father. What joy would be imparted if we said each morning, "God has taken charge of me; He is going with me Himself. I am going to do His will all day in His strength." Yes, what profound peace and power would come if we would continually seek living fellowship with our loving Father.

Reflection

Do you ever get so caught up in religious activities that you forget to focus on God Himself?

How might you enter into "living fellowship" with Him today?

The Blessing of Forgiveness

"Even as Christ forgave you, so you also must do."

Colossians 3:13

Beloved followers of Jesus, called to manifest His likeness to the world, learn that as forgiveness of your sins was one of the first things Jesus did for you, forgiveness of others is one of the first you can do for Him. Remember that there is a joy even sweeter than that of being forgiven—it is the joy of forgiving others.

Thus you can bless the world. As the forgiving one, Jesus has set up His kingdom and continually extends it. Through the same forgiving love, the church will convince the world of God's love. If the world sees men and women loving and forgiving as Jesus did, it will be compelled to confess the truth that God is with them.

To some, forgiveness seems an impossible task—and it is if you rely on your own power. But in union with Christ, we can do it. He who abides in Him walks even as He walked. If you have surrendered yourself to follow Christ in everything, He will by His Holy Spirit enable you to do this, too.

Reflection

What most impresses you about Christ's forgiveness?

Who might you need to forgive, through the power and love of the Holy Spirit?

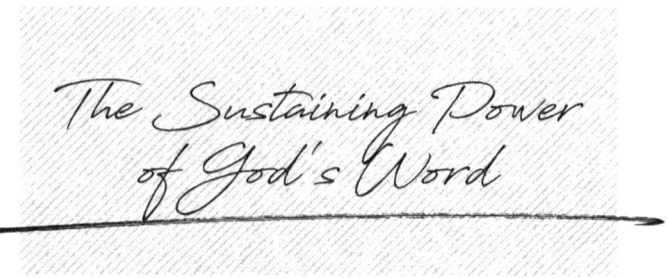

The Sustaining Power of God's Word

"Beginning at Moses and all the Prophets,
[Jesus] expounded to them in all the
Scriptures the things concerning Himself."

Luke 24:27

W hat the Lord Jesus accomplished here on earth as man, He owed greatly to His use of the Scriptures. He found in them the way marked in which He had to walk, the food and the strength by which He could work, the weapon by which He could overcome every enemy. The Scriptures were indeed indispensable to Him through all His life and passion. From beginning to end. His life was the fulfillment of what had been written of Him in the volume of the Book.

It is hardly necessary to produce proofs of this. During the temptation in the wilderness, He conquered Satan by declaring, "It is written" (Matt. 4:4). He continually appealed to the Word: "Have you not even read this Scripture?" and "Is it not written?" (Mark 12:10; 11:17).

He Himself was the living Word. He had the Spirit without measure. If anyone could have done without the written Word, it was Jesus. Yet we see that the Word was everything to Him. More than anyone else, He thus shows us that the life of God in human flesh and the Word of God in human speech are inseparably connected.

The life, thoughts, sentiments, and power of God are embodied in His words. And it is only through His Word that the life of God can really enter into us. His Word is the seed of the heavenly life.

Reflection

To what extent do you rely on God's Word?

What does the Word mean to you day by day?

Trust God to Do His Work in You

"Now He who establishes us with you in
Christ . . . is God."

2 Corinthians 1:21

Many people continually mourn over the vari-
ableness of their spiritual life. Sometimes
there are hours and days of deep earnestness and even blessed experience of Gods grace. But
how little is needed to mar their peace, to bring a cloud
over the soul! And then their faith is shaken. All efforts
to regain their standing appear utterly fruitless, and
neither solemn vows, nor watching and prayer, restore
to them the peace they tasted for a while.

If only they could understand that their own efforts
cause their failure, because God alone can establish us in
Christ Jesus. They should recall that salvation came not
through their own effort and work, but by accepting
God's great gift of grace. Likewise, the first step toward
spiritual growth and vitality is to cease striving and allow
God's Spirit to flow. Being established in Christ day by
day is God's work—a work He delights to do, in spite
of all our weakness and unfaithfulness.

Scripture teaches us that in all God's leading of His
people, faith has always been the one condition of the
manifestation of His power. Faith is the ceasing from all

nature's efforts and all other dependence. Faith is con-
fessed helplessness casting itself on God's promise and
claiming its fulfillment. Faith is putting ourselves quietly
into God's hands for Him to do His work.

Reflection

How easily is your faith shaken?
What is your typical response
when you sense your spiritual
vitality waning?
Is it difficult for you to rest
quietly and let God work in
your life?

Persevering Prayer

"Then He spoke a parable to them, that men
always ought to pray and not lose heart."

Luke 18:1

One of the greatest drawbacks to the life of prayer is the fact that the answer does not come as quickly as we expect. We begin to think, Perhaps I am not praying correctly. So we do not persevere in prayer. Our Lord taught a lesson on this often, and from Him we know that there may be a reason for the delay. The waiting may be a blessing to our souls. Our desire must grow deeper and stronger, and we must ask with our whole heart. God puts us into the practicing school of persevering prayer, so that our weak faith may be strengthened.

Above all, God wants to draw us into closer fellowship with Him. When our prayers are not answered, we learn to realize that the fellowship, nearness, and love of God mean more to us than the answers of our petitions, and we continue in prayer. Listen to this warning: Don't become impatient or discouraged if the answer doesn't come. Continue "steadfastly in prayer" (Rom. 12:12). "Pray without ceasing" (1 Thess. 5:17). Ask whether your prayer is really in accordance with God's will and God's Word. Inquire if it is in the right spirit and in the name of Christ. By continuing to pray, you'll learn that those who have persevered before God are those who have had the greatest power with God in prayer.

Reflection

What blessings have you received through persevering prayer?

How have you responded to the temptation to lose heart and stop praying?

Focus on Jesus

"We all, with unveiled face, beholding as in a
mirror the glory of the Lord, arc being
transformed into the same image from glory
to glory."

2 Corinthians 3:18

Your desire is to be like Christ? Here is the path. Gaze on the glory of God in Him. In Him. That is to say, do not look only to the words, thoughts, and graces in which His glory is seen, but look to Himself—the living, loving Christ. Behold Him, look into His very eye, look into His face, as the loving friend, as the living God.

Look to Him in adoration. Bow before Him as God. His glory has an almighty living power to impart itself to us. Look to Him in faith. Exercise the blessed trust that He is yours, that He has given Himself to you, and that you have a claim to all that is in Him. Look to Him with strong desire. Don't yield to the indifference of the flesh that is satisfied without the full blessing of conformity to the Lord.

It is His purpose to form you into His image. Behold Him with this joyful and certain expectation: The glory I behold in Him is destined for me. As I gaze and wonder and trust, I will become like Christ.

Reflection

Spend quiet moments thinking about Jesus—His glory, His love, what He wants to do in you and through you.

Thank Him for His commitment to work out His image in you.

The Joy of the Lord

"Be glad in the Lord and rejoice."

Psalm 32:11

J oy alone is the proof that what we have really satisfies the heart. As long as duty, self-interest, or other motives influence me, men cannot know what the object of my pursuit or possession is really worth to me. But when it gives me joy, and they see me delight in it, they know that to me at least it is a treasure.

Hence there is nothing so attractive as joy, no preaching so persuasive as the sight of hearts made glad. There is no proof of the reality of God's love and the blessing He bestows as when the joy of God overcomes all the trials of life. And for the Christian's own welfare, joy is no less indispensable. The joy of the Lord is his strength; confidence, courage, and patience find their inspiration in joy. With a heart full of joy, no work can weary and no burden can depress.

If there are times when it comes of itself and the heart feels the unutterable joy of the Saviors presence, praise God for it and seek to maintain it. If at other times feelings are dull and the experience of joy is not such as you wish it, still praise God for the life of unutterable blessedness to which you have been redeemed.

Reflection

What can you do to cultivate joy in your life?

How can you experience the joy that God has for you no matter how challenging your circumstances may be?

Power in the Cross

"For the message of the cross is foolishness
to those who are perishing, but to us who arc
being saved it is the power of God."

1 Corinthians 1:18

W hy aren't there more people who can witness, in the joy of their hearts, that the Spirit of God has possessed them and given them new power to witness for Him? They understand too little of the heart-piercing power of the cross. So the Spirit doesn't have the vessels into which He can pour His fullness.

I bring you a message of joy. The Spirit who is in you, in however limited a measure, is prepared to take you under His teaching, lead you to the cross, and by His heavenly instruction make you know something of what the crucified Christ wills to do for you and in you.

Begin at the beginning. Be faithful in the Inner Chamber. Thank Him that you can count on Him to meet you there. Although everything appears cold, dark, and strained, how in silence before the losing Lord Jesus. Thank the Father that He has given you the Spirit. Be assured that all you do not yet know about your earthly life and eternal life the Spirit of Christ will surely make known to you. Believe that this blessing is for you!

Reflection

Why is the message
of the cross so vital
to our experience of
God's power and
becoming people
into whom He can
pour His blessings?

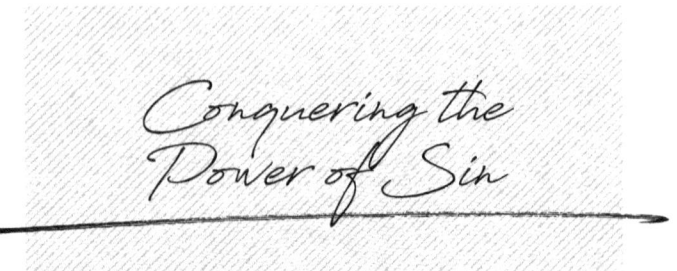

Conquering the Power of Sin

"He who sins is of the devil, for the devil has
sinned from the beginning. For this purpose
the Son of God was manifested, that He
might destroy the works of the devil."

1 John 3:8

One great power of sin is that it blinds men so that they do not recognize its true character. Even the Christian finds an excuse in the thought that he can never be perfect and that some sin is inevitable. He is so accustomed to the thought of sinning that he has almost lost the power and ability to mourn over sin.

Yet there can be no real progress in grace apart from an increased consciousness of the sin and guilt of every transgression against God. There cannot be a more important question than this: "How can I regain the lost tenderness of conscience and really become prepared to offer God the sacrifice of a broken heart?" Scripture teaches us the way. Let the Christian remember what God thinks about sin—the hatred with which His holiness burns against it. Let him remain in God's presence until His holiness shines on him, and he cries out with Isaiah, "Woe is me, for I am undone!" (6:5). Let him take time so that the blood and love of the cross may exercise their full influence on him.

Reflection

When you hear the word sin, what comes to mind?

What is your attitude toward sin?

Why?

In what ways has sin blinded you to its destructive power?

What Will Make Us Holy?

"For I am the Lord your God. You shall
therefore consecrate yourselves, and you shall
be holy; for I am holy."

Leviticus 11:44

In the book of Leviticus, notice how God seven
times commands, "You shall be holy; for I am
holy" (11:44; see also 11:45; 19:2; 20:7, 26; 21:8).
Also repeated is the expression, "I am the Lord who
sanctifies you" (Lev. 20:8; 22:32). This great thought is
carried over into the New Testament. Peter says, "As He
who called you is holy, you also be holy in all your conduct,
because it is written, 'Be holy, for I am holy'" (1 Peter
1:15-16). Paul also writes, "God did not call us to un-
cleanness, but in holiness" (1 Thess. 4:7).

Nothing but the knowledge of God, as the Holy One,
will make us holy. Nowhere can we get to know the
holiness of God, and come under its influence and power,
except in the Inner Chamber. It has been well said, "No
man can expect to make progress in holiness who is not
often and long alone with God."

What is this holiness of God? It is the highest, most
glorious, and most all-embracing of all God's attributes.
Holiness is the most profound word in the Bible. Holiness
is the fire of God that will consume sin in us and make

us holy sacrifices, pure and acceptable before Him. For this reason, the Spirit came down as fire. He is the Spirit of God's holiness, the Spirit of sanctification in us.

Reflection

What is holiness and how is it demonstrated in our lives?

In which areas of your life are your thoughts or actions not holy?

What, according to this reading, can you do to pursue holiness?

Your Biblical Image

"Be doers of the word, and not hearers only."

James 1:22

I n Christ's use of Scripture, the most remarkable thing is this: He found Himself there. He saw there His own image and likeness. And He gave Himself to the fulfillment of what He found written there. This encouraged Him during the bitterest sufferings and strengthened Him for the most difficult work. He had but one thought: to be what the Father had said He should be, to have His life correspond exactly to the image of what He should be as He found it in the Word of God.

Dear Christian, in the Scriptures your likeness is also found, a picture of what the Father desires you to be. Seek to have a deep, clear impression of what the Father says in His Word that you should become. If you fully understand this, it is inconceivable what courage it will give to conquer every difficulty. Go to God's Word each day with the joyful and confident expectation that the Word will accomplish its divine purpose in you.

Nothing makes a man more strong and courageous than the assurance that he is living out the will of God.

Reflection

What is the image of yourself that you see in Scripture?

How is the Bible's image of who God calls you to be different from the way you are right now?

What is your commitment to being who God says you are to be?

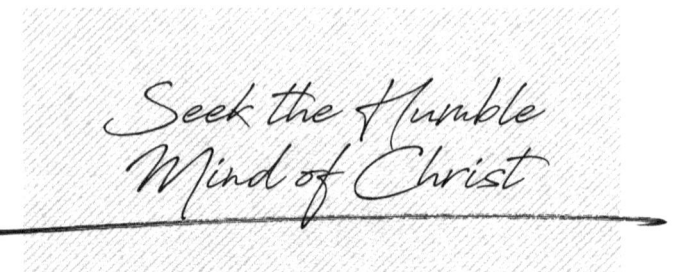

Seek the Humble
Mind of Christ

"Let this mind be in you which was also in
Christ Jesus, who . . . humbled Himself and
became obedient to the point of death, even
the death of the cross."

Philippians 2:5–6,8

W e must be like Christ in His self-emptying
and self-humiliation. The first great act
of self-denial, in which as God He emptied
Himself of His divine glory and power and laid it aside,
was followed up by the no less wondrous humbling of
Himself as man, to the death of the cross.

Does Paul, and do the Scriptures, and does God really
expect this of us? Why not? Or rather, how can they
expect anything else? They know indeed the fearful
power of pride and the old Adam in our nature. But they
also know that Christ has redeemed us not only from the
curse but from the power of sin, and that He gives us
His resurrection life and power to enable us to live as He
did on earth. They say that He is not only our Surety,
but our example, so that we not only live through Him
but live like Him. And further, He is not only our example
but also our Head, who lives in us and continues in us
the life He once led on earth.

With such a Christ, and such a plan of redemption,
can it be otherwise? The follower of Christ must have
the same mind as was in Christ; he must especially be

like Him in His humility.

To attain this, two things are necessary. The first is a fixed purpose and surrender henceforth to be nothing and seek nothing for oneself, but to live only for God and our neighbor. The other is the faith that appropriates the power of Christ's death in this also, as our death to sin and deliverance from its power. Only under the Holy Spirit's teaching and powerful working can one realize, accept, and keep hold of this truth.

Reflection

What is humility, and what impact does it have on our walk with God and our relationships with other people?

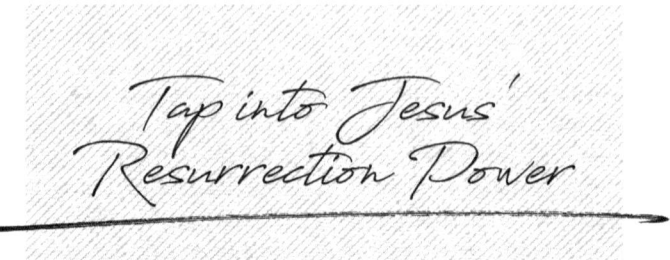

Tap into Jesus' Resurrection Power

"Just as Christ was raised from the dead by the glory of the Father, even so we also should walk in newness of life. For if we have been united together in the likeness of His death, certainly we also shall be in the likeness of His resurrection."

Romans 6:4–5

R aised by the almighty power of God, Jesus' resurrection life was full of the power of eternity. He had not only conquered death and sin for Himself but for His disciples, so that He could . . . make them partakers of His Spirit, His joy, and His heavenly power.

When Jesus makes us partakers of His life, it is not the life He had before His death but the resurrection life He won through death—a life in which sin has already been put away; a life that has already conquered hell and the devil, the world and the flesh; a life of divine power in human nature.

This is the life that likeness to His resurrection gives us: "He died to sin once for all; but the life that He lives, He lives to God. Likewise you also, reckon yourselves to be dead indeed to sin. but alive to God in Christ Jesus our Lord" (Rom. 6:10-11). Oh, that through the Holy Spirit, God might reveal to us the glory of the life in the likeness of Christs resurrection! In it we find the secret of power for a life of conformity to Him.

To most Christians, this is a mystery, and therefore their lives are full of sin, weakness, and defeat. They believe in Christs resurrection as the sufficient proof of their justification. They think He had to rise again to continue His work in heaven as Mediator. But . . . they experience hopelessness when they hear of following Jesus fully and being perfectly conformed to His image . . . They do not know Christ in the power of His resurrection or the mighty power with which His life now works in those who are willing to count all things but loss for His sake (see Phil. 3:8; Eph. 1:19-20).

Reflection

Are you experiencing the joy and power accomplished by Jesus' resurrection?

If you desire the power of the living Christ that can help you face sin and spiritual weakness, ask God to help you realize the complete victory Christ's resurrection accomplished and dedicate yourself to living for Him through the Holy Spirit's power.

A Life of Service

"Through love serve one another."

Galatians 5:13

To the question, how far are we to go in living for, in loving, in serving, in saving men, the Scriptures do not hesitate to give the unequivocal answer: We are to go as far as Jesus, even to the laying down of our lives.

How clearly this comes out in the words of the Master Himself: "Whoever desires to become great among you shall be your servant. And whoever of you desires to be first shall be slave of all. For even the Son of Man did not come to be served, but to serve" (Mark 10:43-45).

Let us pray for the light of the Holy Spirit to show us this, until we learn to feel that we are in the world just as Christ was, to give up self, to love and serve, to live and die . . . Oh, that God would enable His people to know their calling; that they do not belong to themselves, but to God and their fellow men . . .

As we wait for Christ to work out His likeness, as we trust the Holy Spirit to give His mind in us more perfectly, let us in faith begin at once to act as followers of Him who only lived and died to be a blessing to others.

Reflection

When you hear the word serve, what immediately comes to mind?

Why?

Think about someone who has served you and the impact he or she had on your life.

The Influence of Christlike Obedience

"As the Father loved Me. I also have loved you; abide in My love. If you keep My commandments, you will abide in My love, just as I have kept My Father's commandments and abide in His love."

John 15:9-10

O h, if the Christian would but take time to let this wondrous thought fill him: "I am the Beloved of the Lord; Jesus loves me even moment, just as the Father loved Him," how the faith would grow . . .

Christlike obedience is the way to a Christlike enjoyment of Love divine. How it secures our boldness of access into God's presence! "Let us not love in word or in tongue, but in deed and in truth" (1 John 3:18). "Beloved, if our heart does not condemn us, we have confidence toward God. And whatever we ask we receive from Him, because we keep His commandments and do those things that are pleasing in His sight" (1 John 3:21-22). How it gives us boldness before men, and lifts us above their approval or contempt, because we move at God's bidding and feel that we have but to obey orders! And what boldness, too, in the face of difficulty or danger! We are doing God's will and dare leave to Him all responsibility as to failure or success. The heart filled with the thought of direct and entire obedience to God alone rises above the world into the will of God, into the place where God's love rests on him. Like Christ, he has his abode in the love of God.

Let us seek to learn from Christ what it means to have this spirit of obedience ruling our life. It implies the spirit of dependence; the confession that we have neither the right nor the desire in anything to do our own will. It involves teachableness of spirit. Conscious of the binding influence of tradition, prejudice, and habit, it takes its law not from men but from God Himself.

Reflection

Why does obeying God give us boldness in the face of difficulty or danger?

What happens when believers pay more attention to human traditions and habits than they do to God's will?

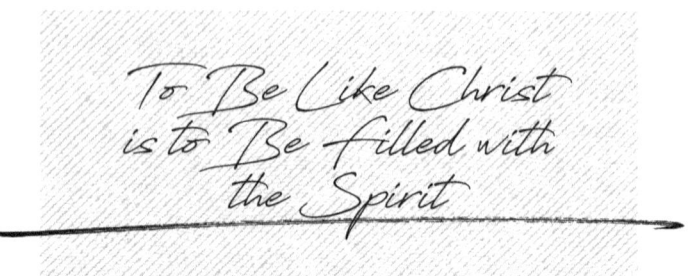

To Be Like Christ
is to Be filled with
the Spirit

"Be filled with the Spirit."

Ephesians 5:18

Jesus, who was baptized with the Spirit to set us an example of how to live, has ascended into heaven to baptize us in the likeness of Himself. The person who would live like Christ must begin here—he must be baptized with the Spirit. What God demands from His children, He first gives. He demands entire likeness to Christ because He will give us, as He did Jesus, the fullness of the Spirit. We must be filled with the Spirit.

We have here the reason why teaching concerning the imitation and likeness to Christ has so little prominence in the church of Christ. Men sought it in their own strength, with the help of some workings of the Holy Spirit. They did not understand that nothing less was needed than being filled with the Spirit. No wonder they thought that real conformity to Christ could not be expected of us; they had mistaken thoughts about being filled with the Spirit. It was thought to be the privilege of a few, not the calling and duty of every child of God. It was not sufficiently realized that "be filled with the Spirit" is a command given to every Christian.

Only when the church first gives the baptism of the Spirit, and Jesus—the Savior who, with the Spirit, baptizes each person who believes in Him—will people seek after their rightful place and attain likeness to Christ. They will then understand and acknowledge that to be like Christ, they must be led by the same Spirit; and to be led by the Spirit, as He was, they must be filled with the Spirit. Nothing less than the fullness of the Spirit is absolutely necessary to live a truly Christian, Christlike life.

Reflection

What exactly does it mean to be "filled with the Spirit"?

In what ways do Christians sometimes hinder the work of the Spirit in their lives?

Ask God to fill you with His Spirit today.

Glorify God in Everything

"I have glorified You on the earth. I have
finished the work which You have given Me
to do."

John 17:4

Beloved Christian, is it not a wonderful calling, blessed beyond all conception, to live as Christ did only to glorify God, to let Gods glory shine out in every part of our lists? Let us take time to take in this wondrous thought: Our daily lives, down to their most ordinary acts, may be transparent with the glory of God. Oh, let us study this trait as one that makes the wondrous image of our Jesus especially attractive to us. He glorified the Father. Let us listen to Him as He points us to the high aim, that our Father in heaven may be glorified, and as He shows us the way, "By this My Father is glorified."

Let our whole life, like Christ's, be animated by this as its ruling principle, growing stronger until in a holy enthusiasm our watchword has become: ALL, ALL TO THE GLORY OF GOD. And let our faith hold last the confidence that in the fullness of the Spirit there is the certain provision for our desire being fulfilled: "Do you not know that your body is the temple of the Holy Spirit? . . . Therefore glorify God in your body and in your spirit" (1 Cor. 6:19-20) . . .

Let simple, downright obedience mark our whole life. Let a humble, childlike waiting for direction, a soldier-like looking for orders, a Christlike dependence on the Fathers showing us the way, be our daily attitude. Let everything be done for the Lord, according to His will, for His glory, in direct relationship to Him. Let Gods glory shine out in the holiness of our life.

Reflection

What are some practical ways in which you can fulfill your calling to glorify God today?

Waiting on God for Guidance

"Show me Your ways, O Lord; teach me Your paths. Lead me in Your truth and teach me, for You are the God of my salvation; on You I wait all the day."

Psalm 25:4-5

The Father in heaven so longs to have His child's life at every step in His wall and His love that He is willing to keep the child's guidance entirely in His own hand. He knows so well that we are unable to do what is really holy and heavenly except as He works it in us. He desires His demands to become promises of what He will do. Not only during special difficulties and times of perplexity, but during the common course of everyday life, we can count on Him to teach us His way and show us His path.

What is needed in order for us to receive this guidance? One thing: waiting for instructions from God. During our times of prayer, we want to clearly express our sense of need, and our faith in His help. We definitely want to become conscious of what God's way may be and our need for divine light upon our path. We want to wait quietly before God in prayer until the deep, restful assurance fills us.

Reflection

Do you really believe God loves you, watches over you, and wants to lead you through each day?

How is your view of God influencing the way in which you approach Him in prayer?

Live Life Through the Power of Jesus

"That you may know . . . what are the riches
of the glory of His inheritance in the saints,
and what is the exceeding greatness of His
power toward us who believe, according to
the working of His mighty power."

Ephesians 1:18–19

C hrist calls you to a life of faith and dependence
because it is the life He led. He has tried it and
proved its blessedness. He is willing to live
over again His life in you, to teach you to live in no other
way. He knew that the Father was His life, that He lived
through the Father, and that the Father supplied His
need moment by moment. Now He assures you that as
He lived through the Father, you shall live through Him.

Take this assurance in faith. Let your heart be filled
with the thought of the blessedness of this fullness of
life, which is prepared for you in Christ and will be abundantly supplied as you need it. Don't think any more of
your spiritual life as something you must watch over with
anxiety. Rejoice every day that you don't need to live on
your own strength but in your Lord Jesus.

Believer, Jesus' divine power will work in and through
us. Don't think that your earthly circumstances make a
holy life to Gods glory impossible. Christ came and lived
on earth to manifest the divine life, in the midst of earthly
surroundings that were even more difficult. As Jesus

lived so blessed an earthly life through the Father, so you can also live your earthly life through Him. Cultivate large expectations of what the Lord will do for you. Let it be your sole desire to attain a full union with Him.

Reflection

In what ways are you appropriating Christs power and living life in His strength?
In what areas do you need more of His strength to live more fully and fruitfully?

Committed to Christ

"Moses the man of God blessed the children
of Israel."

Deuteronomy 33:1

"**T**he man of God!" How much this phrase means! A man who comes from God, chosen and sent by Him. A man who walks with God, lives in His fellowship, and carries the mark of His presence. A man who lives for God and His will, whose whole being is pervaded and ruled by the glory of God, who involuntarily and unceasingly leads men to think of God.

The world needs such men of God. He seeks such men, that He may fill them with Himself and send them into the world to help others know Him. Moses was so distinctly such a man that men naturally spoke of him as "Moses the man of God." Every servant of the Lord ought to aim at being such a man—a living witness and proof of what God is to him in heaven and on earth.

These are the men the world and God equally need. Why? Because the world, by sin, has fallen away from God. Because in Christ the world has been redeemed for God. Man was created for God, that God might live, dwell, work, and show forth His glory in him and through him.

Reflection

Are you fully committed to God, living for Him and desiring to lead other people to Him?

How might you more fully reflect God's glory in your life?

Living by Dying to Self

"For we who live are always delivered to
death for Jesus' sake, that the life of Jesus
also may be manifested in our mortal flesh."

2 Corinthians 4:11

The cross means the death of self—the utter surrender of our own will and life to be lost in the will of God. This is what the cross meant to Jesus. It cost Him a terrible struggle before He could give Himself up to it. When He was troubled and deeply distressed, it was because His whole being shrank back from that cross and its curse. Three times He had to pray before He could fully say, "Not My will, but Yours, be done." By doing so, He was saying, "Let Me do anything, rather than God's will not being done. I give up everything—only God's will must be done."

We who seek to live like Christ must also relinquish ourselves to God, that we might learn to be and do nothing but His will. Realizing that we have not the ability to think or do anything good or bad within our own power, we must be willing to submit even faculty of body, soul, and spirit to Jesus. The distrust of self in everything and the trust of Jesus in everything are what enable us to do the will of God. Then the very spirit of the cross breathes through our whole being.

Reflection

Are you committed to doing only God's will, yielding every part of Yourself to Jesus in order to experience the resurrection life?

If not, what are you keeping back?

Love Motivates

"For this is the love of God, that we keep His commandments."

1 John 5:3

Our profession of love is worthless except as it is proved to be true by the keeping of God's commandments. Knowing God, having the love of God perfected in us, having boldness with God, and abiding in Him—all is dependent on one thing: keeping the commandments.

It is only as we realize the prominence Christ and Scripture give to this truth that we will learn to give it the same prominence in our life. It will become to us one of the keys of true Bible study. The person who reads his Bible with the longing and determined purpose to search out and obey every commandment of God is sure to receive all the blessings of the Word. He will especially learn two things: how he needs to wait for the teaching of the Holy Spirit to lead him into all God's will and what blessedness there is in performing daily duties for Christ's sake.

The question is to be decided whether you will seek to keep Christ's commandments every day. And there, too, will be decided whether in future life you will bear the character of a person wholly given up to know and do God's will.

Reflection

How will you live today . . . and tomorrow?

What may be keeping you from finding and obeying God's commandments— and receiving the full blessings God desires to give you?

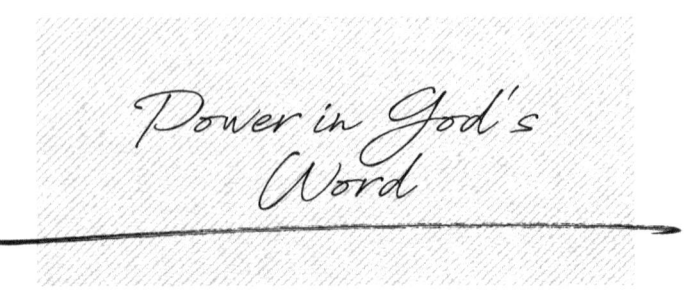

Power in God's Word

"Let the word of Christ dwell in you richly."

Colossians 3:16

One of the first requisites to fruitful Bible study is the recognition of God as the omnipotent one and of the power of His Word. The psalmist wrote, "By the word of the Lord the heavens were made . . . He spoke, and it was done; He commanded, and it stood fast" (33:6,9).

As the Word of the living God, it is a living Word and gives life. It cannot only call into existence, but even make alive again that which is dead. Its quickening power can raise dead bodies, giving eternal life to dead souls. All spiritual life comes through it, because we are born ol incorruptible seed by the Word of God that lives and abides forever.

Here lies, hidden from many, one of the deepest secrets of the blessing of God's Word—the faith in its creative and quickening energy. The Word will work in me the very disposition or grace that it commands or promises. Everything depends on learning the art of receiving that Word into the heart. And in learning this art, the first step is developing firm faith in its living, omnipotent, creative power.

Reflection

What does it mean
to your daily life
that God's Word is
"living"?

What do you
understand about
the power of God's
Word?

How Do You Know God?

"You shall love the Lord your God with all
your heart . . . and with all your mind."

Matthew 22:37

There are two ways of knowing things. The one is in the mind by notion or conception: I know about something. The other is in the life: I know by inward experience. A blind man, who is wise and clever, may know all that science teaches about light by having books read to him. A child, or an unlearned person, may never have thought about what light is, yet knows it far better than the blind scholar. One knows about it by thinking; the other knows it in reality by seeing and enjoying it.

So it is with spiritual matters. The mind can form thoughts about God from the Bible and know all the doctrines of salvation, while the inner life doesn't know God's power to save. This is why we read, "He who does not love does not know God, for God is love" (1 John 4:8). He may know all about God's love and be able to utter beautiful things about it. But unless he loves, he doesn't know God. Only love can know God. The knowledge of God is life eternal.

Only the experience and possession of God and His goodness give true knowledge. The knowledge of the intellect cannot give life. We need the intellect to hear and understand God's Word in its human meaning. But we need to know that the possession of the truth by intellect can only profit as the Holy Spirit makes it life and truth in the heart. We need to yield our heart and wait on God in quiet submission. As this becomes a holy habit, we'll learn the art of intellect and heart working in perfect harmony. Each movement of the mind will be accompanied by a corresponding movement of the heart, waiting on and listening for the teaching of the Spirit.

Reflection

Think about the difference between knowing about God and knowing God. Which one most closely fits you?

What role does the Holy Spirit have in bringing the mind and heart together during the study of God's Word?

Don't Trust Your Own Spiritual Understanding

"Trust in the Lord with all your heart, and
lean not on your own understanding."

Proverbs 3:5

W hy do many believers find Bible teaching
and Bible study relatively fruitless? Why
does the church often lack the fullness of
power, devotion, and holiness it could enjoy? The answer
is found in the Proverb above: Christians too often rely
on their own understanding.

Many argue, "Surely God gave us our intellect, and
without it there's no possibility of knowing God's Word."
That's true, but listen. By the fall, our whole human
nature was disordered. The will became enslaved, affections were perverted, understanding was darkened. All
people admit the ruin of the fall in the two former, but
practically deny it in the latter. To think we can take
knowledge of God's truth for ourselves out of His Word
as we will is still our greatest danger. We need a deep
conviction of the impotence of our understanding really
to know the truth and of the terrible danger of self-
confidence and self-deception.

It is only with the heart that we can know God, and
worship God, in spirit and truth. In the heart, therefore,
the divine Word does the work. Into our heart, God has

sent the Spirit of His Son. It is the heart—the inward life of desire, love, will, and surrender—that the Holy Spirit guides into all the truth.

Instead of relying on your understanding, come with your heart to the Bible. Instead ol trusting your understanding, trust in the Lord with all your heart. With every thought from the Word that your understanding grasps, bow before God in dependence and trust. Ask the Holy Spirit to make it work effectively in your heart.

Reflection

When you study the Bible, how much unity is there between your heart and your mind? Ask God to lead you into His truth, for the Holy Spirit to guide your understanding and protect you from self-deception.

Abiding in Christ

"And now . . . abide in Him."

1 John 2:28

God's providence places many Christians in business, where for hours at a time they are required to pay the closest attention to the work they have to do. How can such a man, it is asked, with his whole mind focused on his work, be at the same time occupied with Christ and keep up fellowship with Him?

Abiding in Jesus is not a work for which the mind needs to be occupied each moment or the emotions to be directly and actively engaged. It is an entrusting of oneself to the keeping of the eternal love, in the faith that it will abide near us, and with its holy presence watch over us—even when we must be intently occupied with other things.

Think of a king: In the midst of work, pleasure, and trial, he all the while acts under the secret influence of the consciousness of royalty, even while he does not think about it. A loving wife and mother never for one moment loses the sense of her relationship to her husband and children; the consciousness and the love are there, amidst all her responsibilities. Our abiding in Jesus is even more than a fellowship of love—it is a fellowship of life. In work or in rest, the consciousness of life never leaves us. And likewise, the mighty power of the eternal life can maintain within us the consciousness of its presence. Or rather, Christ, who is our life, dwells within us and by His presence maintains our consciousness that we are in Him.

Reflection

How might your life be different if you entrust yourself every day to God and live life with an awareness of His presence with you?

Depend on God

"I thank You, Father, Lord of heaven and
earth, that You have hidden these things from
the wise and prudent and have revealed them
to babes."

Matthew 11:25

All evangelical Christians believe in regeneration. How few believe that when a man is born of God, a babe-like dependence on God for all teaching and strength ought to be his chief characteristic. It was the one thing our Lord Jesus insisted on above all. Why did He pronounce the poor in heart, the meek, and the hungry "blessed"? Why did He call men to learn that He was meek and lowly in heart? Why did He speak so often of humbling ourselves and becoming as little children? Because the chief mark of being a child of God is an absolute dependence on God for even blessing, and especially for any real knowledge of spiritual things.

Live as a babe before God. As a newborn babe, desire the milk of the Word. Beware of trying to assume this state of mind only when you want to study Scripture. It must be the permanent habit of your mind, the state of your heart. Then alone can you enjoy the continual guidance of the Holy Spirit.

Reflection

What did Murray mean by a "babe-like dependence on God"?

How is this attitude different from the way many Christians approach God?

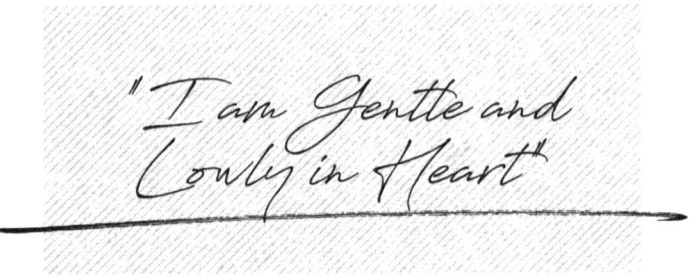

"I am Gentle and Lowly in Heart"

"Take My yoke upon you and learn from Me,
for I am gentle and lowly in heart, and you
will find rest for your souls."

Matthew 11:29

Our Lord here opens up the innermost secret of His inner life. That which He brought down to us from heaven, that which equipped Him to be a teacher and Savior, that which He wants us to learn of Him, you find it all in these words: "I am gentle and lowly in heart." It is the one virtue that makes Him the Lamb of God, our suffering Redeemer, heavenly Teacher, and Leader. It is the one disposition that He asks of us in coming to learn from Him.

As a learner, you must come, study, and believe in Him—the gentle and lowly one—and seek to learn from Him how to be meek and lowly too.

This is the root of the Christian life: to be nothing before God and men; to wait on God alone; to delight in, to imitate, to learn of Christ, the gentle and lowly one. This is the very key to the School of Christ, the only key to the true knowledge of Scripture. It is in this character that Christ has come to teach; it is in this character alone you can learn of Him. Humility, the meek and lowly heart, has had little place in the Christian church and the teachings of God's Word. I am deeply persuaded that this lack lies at the root of the feebleness and unfruitfulness of which we hear. It is only as we are gentle and lowly in heart that Christ can teach us by His Spirit what God has for us.

Reflection

How highly do you value humility?

How responsive are you to what God wants to teach you about being "gentle and lowly in heart"?

What have you learned through humility that you could learn no other way?

Spiritual Understanding

"For as the heavens are higher than the earth,
so are My ways higher than your ways, and
My thoughts than your thoughts."

Isaiah 55:9

God's Word has two meanings. One is that which it has in the mind of God, making human words the bearer of all the glory of divine wisdom, power, and love. The other is our feeble, partial, defective understanding of it. Even after grace and experience have made such words as the love of God, salvation, redemption, and other spiritual concepts true and real to us, there is still an infinite fullness in the Word we have not yet known.

Even when the Word has spoken God's thoughts, and our thoughts have sought to take them in, they remain as high above our thoughts as the heavens are higher than the earth. All the infinities of God and the eternal world dwell in the Word as the seed of eternal life.

The Holy Spirit is already in us to reveal the things of God. In answer to our humble believing prayer, God will give ever-growing insight into the spiritual mysteries—our wonderful union and likeness to Christ, His living in us, and our being as He was in this world.

Reflection

Pray that the Holy Spirit will give you insights into God's thoughts and mysteries.

The next time you read a portion of Scripture, ask God to open your understanding of Him and His living Word.

Press On

"In the world you will have tribulation; but be
of good cheer, I have overcome the world."

John 16:33

I f the church of Christ were what it should be—
if older believers were encouraging younger
converts to persist and persevere amidst all hardships—abiding in Christ would come as the natural out-
growth of being in Him. But in the sickly state in which
such a great part of the church is, people who are pressing after this blessing are sorely hindered by the depress-
ing influence of the thought and life around them.

I don't say this to discourage but to warn—and to
urge us to cast ourselves more entirely on the Word of
God Himself. There may come more than one hour in
which you are ready to yield to despair, but be of good
courage. Only believe. He who has put the blessing within
your reach will assuredly lead to its possession. Day by
day, amidst discouragement and difficulty, we have to
press forward.

Reflection

In which areas of
life do you need
God's
encouragement?

What might you do
to help encourage
another believer?

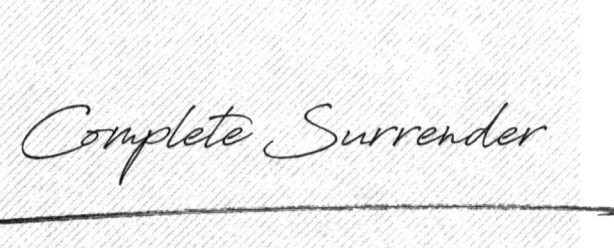

Complete Surrender

"And we are His witnesses of these things;
and so is also the Holy Ghost, whom God
hath given to them that obey Him."

Acts 5:32

When the Lord Jesus promised the Spirit to His disciples, it was with the full expectation that they would yield themselves fully to the leading and power of the Spirit. It is with the same expectation that the Spirit will be granted anew each day, if we yield ourselves unreservedly to be sanctified in all our actions and conversation. Oh, that our eyes were open to see how right and how blessed this is!

Many Christians pray for the Holy Spirit but always with a certain reservation, because they intend in many things to continue doing their own will. Christian, when you pray, entrust yourself fully to the guidance of the Holy Spirit for the whole day. If there is true willingness on your part, the Holy Spirit will take full possession of you and will preserve and sanctify your life.

Don't serve God halfheartedly. Pray for the enlightenment of the Spirit, that you may see the possibility and the blessedness of a life fully surrendered to His service.

Reflection

Think about whether or not you are being led and guided each day by the Holy Spirit.

What are your reservations in praying for the Holy Spirits guidance?

Bring Your Needs Before God

"Oh, give thanks to the Lord! Call upon His
name; make known His deeds among the
peoples! . . . Seek the Lord and His strength;
seek His face evermore!"

Psalm 105:1, 4

Can it be true, as so many people complain, that there is no time for communion with God? Is not the most important matter fellowship with God, in which we may experience His love and power? I urge you to make time with God your highest priority.

You need time to feed on the Word of God and draw from it life for your soul. Through His Word, His thoughts and His grace enter our hearts and lives. Take time each day to read the Bible, even if it be only a few verses. Meditate on what you have read, and thus assimilate the bread of life. If you do not take the time to let God speak to you through His Word, how can you expect to be led by the Spirit?

Meditate on the Word and lay it before God in prayer as the pledge of what He will do for you. The Word gives you matter for prayer and power in prayer. Our prayers are often futile because we speak our own thoughts and have not taken time to hear what God has to say.

It is of little use to speak of the deeper, more abundant life of Christ if we do not daily, above all things, take time for communication with our Father. The life, love, and holiness of God cannot be ours amidst the world's distractions and temptations unless we give Him time to reveal Himself to us and take possession of our hearts.

Reflection

What specific steps can you take, starting today, to spend more time in communion with God?

Which distractions and temptations have you allowed to reduce your time with God?

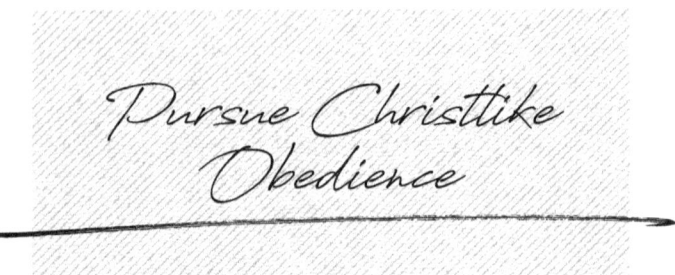

Pursue Christlike Obedience

"Blessed are those who hear the word of God
and keep it!"

Luke 11:28

Child of God, one of the first marks of conformity to Christ is obedience—simple and implicit obedience to all the will of God. Begin by willingly and wholeheartedly keeping every one of the commands of God's holy Word. Go on to a very tender yielding to everything that conscience tells you to be right, even when the Word does not directly command it.

A hearty obedience to the commandments and a ready submission to conscience wherever it speaks are the preparation for that divine teaching of the Spirit that will lead you deeper into the meaning of the Word and understanding of God's will. And if it ever appears too hard to live only for God's will, let us remember where Christ found His strength: Because it was the Father's will, the Son rejoiced to do it. As He said, "This command I have received from my Father" (John 10:18).

Let it be our chief desire to say each day, "I am the Father's beloved child" and to think of each commandment as the Fathers will. A Christlike sense of sonship will lead to a Christlike obedience.

Reflection

Why do so many
people today rail
against God's
commandments?

Why is it important
to remember that
the commandments
are the Father's will
for you —His
beloved child?

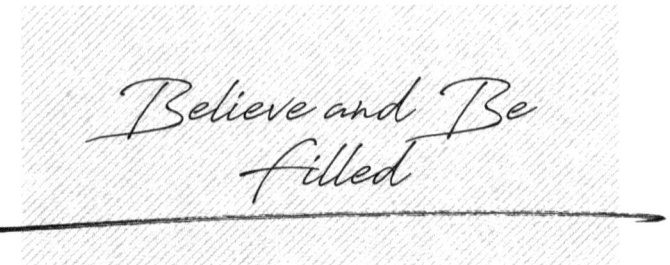

Believe and Be Filled

"The anointing which you have received from
Him abides in you."

1 John 2:27

Believe that as surely as you dwell in Christ, you have His Spirit dwelling in you, too. Believe that He will do His work with power, if only you do not hinder Him. Believe that He is working, even when you cannot discern it. Believe that He will work mightily if you ask this from the Father. Believe that the fullness of the Spirit is indeed your daily portion. It is impossible to live the life of full abiding without being full of the Holy Spirit.

Be sure to take time in prayer to dwell at the footstool of the throne of God and the Lamb, from which flows the river of life. It is there, and only there, that you can be filled with the Spirit. Cultivate carefully the habit of daily—yes, continually—honoring Him by the quiet, restful confidence that He is doing His work within. Let faith in His indwelling make you jealous of whatever could grieve Him—the spirit of the world or the actions of self and the flesh. Let that faith seek its nourishment in the Word and all it says about the Spirit.

The Holy Spirit was given for this one purpose—that the glorious redemption and life in Christ might with divine power be conveyed and communicated to us. We have the Holy Spirit to make the living Christ, in all His saving power and in the completeness of His victory over sin, ever present in us

Reflection

What does the Holy Spirit desire to do within you?

Why is it so important to believe in His ongoing work within you?

Obey God's Word

"If you know these things, blessed are you if
you do them."

John 13:17

There is no blessedness in hearing or knowing
God's Word apart from keeping it. The Word
is nothing if it is not kept, obeyed, done. "If
anyone wills to do His will, he shall know" (John 7:17).
According to this saying of our Lord, all true knowledge
of God's Word depends on there being first the will to do it.

Why this should be so is easily ascertained when we
think about what words are meant for. They stand between the will and the deed. A man wills to do something
for you; before he does it, he expresses his thought or
purpose in words. Then he fulfills the words by doing
what he has promised. Even so with God. His words have
their value from what He does. The truth and the worth
of what God promises consists in this— that He does it.

This is no less true of His words of command and
instruction. If we study them to gain knowledge, if we
admire their beauty and praise their wisdom, but do not
do them, we delude ourselves. They are meant to be done.
It is only as we do them that their real meaning and
blessing can be unfolded to us. It is only as we do them
that we really can grow in the divine life.

Reflection

Why is it important
to do what God's
Word tells you to
do?

In which areas of
your life do you
hesitate to obey God
completely?

The Fruit of Affliction

"I am the true vine, and My Father is the vinedresser. Every branch in Me that does not bear fruit He takes away; and every branch that bears fruit He prunes, that it may bear more fruit."

John 15:1-2

During a storm, the tree strikes deeper roots into the soil. During a hurricane, the inhabitants of the house abide within and rejoice in its shelter. Likewise, the Father would lead us, through adversity and affliction, to enter more deeply into the love of Christ.

Our hearts are continually prone to wander from Him. Prosperity and enjoyment all too easily satisfy us, dull our spiritual perception, and hinder us from full communion with Him. It is an unspeakable mercy that the Father comes with His chastisement, makes the world around us dark and unattractive, leads us to feel our sinfulness more deeply, and for a time lose our joy in what was becoming so dangerous. He does it in the hope that, when we have found refuge in Christ amidst trouble, we will learn to seek Him first and abide in Him at all times. When the affliction is removed, we will have grown so firmly into Him that during prosperity He still will be our only joy.

Of each vine, the vinedresser is continually asking how it can bring forth more fruit. Believer, abide in Christ during times of affliction and you will bring forth more fruit. The deeper experience of Christ's tenderness and the Fathers love will urge you to live to His glory. The surrender of self during suffering will prepare you to sympathize with the misery of others, while the softening that results from chastisement will fit you for becoming, as Jesus was, the servant of all. The thought of the Fathers desire for fruit in the pruning will lead you to yield yourself afresh to Him.

Reflection

In what ways has suffering strengthened your relationship with God?

How has it made you more sensitive to the needs of other people?

Why does God sometimes allow suffering in our lives?

Filled for a Purpose

"But when He, the Spirit of truth, has come,
He will guide you into all truth . . . He will
glorify Me."

John 16:13–14

W e seek sometimes the operation of the Spirit so that we might obtain more power for work, more love in the life, more holiness in the heart, more light on Scripture or on our path. Yet all these gifts are only subordinate to God's great purpose. The Father has bestowed the Spirit on the Son, and the Son has given Him to us, with the one great object of revealing and glorifying Christ Jesus Himself in us.

The heavenly Christ must become for us a real, living personality, always with us and in us. Our life on earth must be lived every day in the unbroken and holy fellowship of our Lord Jesus in heaven. This must be the first and greatest work of the Holy Spirit in believers—that they should know and experience Christ as the life of their life. God desires that we should become strengthened with might by His Spirit, that Christ may dwell in our hearts through faith, and that we may be filled with His love.

This was the secret of the first disciples' joy. They had received the Lord Jesus, whom they feared they had

240

lost, as the heavenly Christ into their hearts. This was their preparation for Pentecost: They were entirely taken up with Him. Their hearts were empty of everything, so that the Spirit might fill them with Christ. In the fullness of the Spirit, they had power for a life and service such as the Lord desired. Is this, now, with us, the great object in our desires, in our prayers, in our experience?

Reflection

Why has Jesus given us the Holy Spirit?

How seriously do you desire the full indwelling of the Holy Spirit?

The Prayer God Blesses

"Praying always with all prayer and
supplication in the Spirit, being watchful to
this end with all perseverance and
supplication for all the saints."

Ephesians 6:18

P rayer in our own strength brings no blessing. Take time to present yourself reverently and in quietness before God. Remember His greatness, holiness, and love. Think over what you wish to ask from Him. Do not be satisfied with going over the same things every day. No child goes on saying the same thing day after day to his earthly father.

Conversation with the Father is colored by the needs of the day. Let your prayer be something definite, arising either out of the Word that you have read or out ol the real soul-needs you long to have satisfied. Let your prayer be so definite that you can say, "I know what I have asked from my Father, and I expect an answer." It is a good plan sometimes to take a piece ol paper and write down what you wish to pray for. You might keep such a paper for a week or more and repeat the prayers until some new need arises.

One great reason why prayer does not bring more joy and blessing is that it is too selfish, and selfishness is the death of prayer. Remember your family, your neighbors, and the church to which you belong. Let your heart be enlarged, and pray on behalf of the church throughout the world. Become an intercessor, and you will experience the blessedness ol prayer as you find out that God will use you to share His blessing with others through prayer. You will begin to feel that there is something worth living for, as you find that you have something to say to God, and that He will do mighty things in answer to your prayers that otherwise would not have been done.

Reflection

How might your prayer life become more vibrant and rich?

Who might God wish for you to pray for regularly?

What blessings of prayer have you experienced?

Our Waiting Is Not in Vain

"Wait on the Lord; be of good courage, and
He shall strengthen your heart; wait, I say, on
the Lord!"

Psalm 27:14

O ne of the chief needs in our waiting on God,
one of the deepest secrets of its blessedness
and blessing, is a quiet, confident persuasion
that it is not in vain. We need courage to believe that
God will hear and help. We are waiting on a God who
never could disappoint His people.

"Be strong and of good courage." These words are
frequently connected with some great and difficult en-
terprise, in anticipation of combat with the power of
strong enemies and the utter insufficiency of all human
strength. Is waiting on God so difficult that such words
are needed? Yes, indeed.

When we determine to wait on God, we ought
beforehand to resolve that it will be with the most confident expectation that God will meet and bless us. We
ought to make up our minds on this—that nothing was
ever so sure as that waiting on God will bring us untold
and unexpected blessing.

Wait on God to know first who He is and then what
He will do. The whole duty and blessedness of waiting

on God has its root in this—that He is such a blessed Being that we cannot ever come into contact with Him without His life, goodness, and power permeating our hearts and lives.

Reflection

Do you expect God to meet you and bless you when you wait on Him?

Why or why not?

What can you do to remind yourself of God's great promises to you?

Prayer and God's Word

"We will give ourselves continually to prayer
and to the ministry of the word."

Acts 6:4

P rayer and the Word are inseparably linked
together; power in the use of one depends on
the presence of the other. The Word shows
me the path of prayer, telling me how God would have
me act. It gives me the power for prayer, the assurance
that I will be heard. And it brings me the answer to
prayer, as it teaches what God will do for me. In turn,
prayer prepares the heart for receiving the Word from
God Himself, for the teaching of the Spirit to give spiritual
understanding.

It is clear why this is so. Prayer and the Word have
one common center—God. Prayer seeks God; the Word
reveals God. In prayer, man asks God; in the Word, God
answers man. In prayer, man rises to heaven to dwell
with God; in the Word, God comes to dwell with man.
In prayer, man gives himself to God; in the Word, God
gives Himself to man. Prayer and the Word will be a
blessed fellowship with God, the interchange of thought
and love and life, a dwelling in God and God in us. Seek
God and live!

Reflection

Do you use Gods Word as a basis for your prayers?

How might your prayer life be strengthened if you incorporated the Bible more often?

A Love Beyond Comprehension

"Who shall separate us from the love of Christ?"

Romans 8:35

G od is love. Love is His very being. Love is not an attribute, but the very essence of His nature, the center around which all His glorious attributes gather. It was because He was love that He was the Father, and that there was a Son. Love needs an object to whom it can give itself away, in whom it can lose itself, with whom it can make itself one. Because God is love, there must be a Father and a Son. The love of the Father toward the Son is that divine passion with which He delights in the Son and speaks, "My beloved Son, in whom I am well pleased" (Matt. 17:5).

When we gather together all the attributes of God—His infinity, His perfection. His immensity, His majesty, His omnipotence—and consider them but as the rays of the glory of His love, we still fail in forming any conception of what that love must be. It is a love that transcends all understanding.

Yet this love of God toward His Son must serve as the glass in which you are to learn how Jesus loves you. As one of His redeemed children, you are His delight. All of His desire is toward you, with the longing of a love that is stronger than death and that many waters cannot quench (Song 8:6-7). His heart yearns after you, seeking your fellowship and your love. Were it needed, He would die again to possess you. As the Father loved the Son, and could not live without Him, so Jesus loves you. His life is bound up in yours; you are to Him inexpressibly more indispensable and precious than you ever can know.

Reflection

Meditate on Jesus' deep love for you, a love so great that He came to earth and died on the cross for the sins of humankind.

He longs to be in fellowship with you and considers you His precious child!

Subject Index

Christlikeness

Church

Community

Compassion

Cross

Dependence on God

If you have enjoyed this book, look out for these other additions to the series for sale online:

The Best of George MacDonald
The Best of Jonathan Edwards
The Best of Robert Murray McCheyne
The Best of F. B. Meyer
The Best of E. M. Bounds
The Best of Charles Spurgeon
The Best of D. L. Moody

If this book has impacted your life, we would love to hear from you.
Please contact us at info@honorbooks.com